UGLY DUCKLING PRESSE

STUDY

STUDY

& Other Poems on Art

Yuko Otomo

TABLE OF CONTENTS

YUKO OTOMO : DICHOTOMY'S GRACE

It is not easy to make dichotomy. Usually, it ends up stale, with no rhythm, no verve. In Yuko Otomo's poems for Robert Frank, reacting to his depictions of the pimples and warts of Americana, she writes, "As cheers fill the streets, / a new sense of HUNGER / nails the interior darkness down." One wonders what she, born in Japan, learns from him, born in Switzerland. The foreigner sees with sharper eye, smells with sharper nose. Yet the poet abjures the senses working in the metaphysic her art commands.

A little later in the same sequence, she comes back to the idea of a dark interior:

Let's fool ourselves thinking
it's not drinks that we want,
but the shaded interior
of "somewhere" where
the sun doesn't reveal
the details of our lives
too cruelly.

That cruelty recurs in the poems, as a nagging unnecessary part of existence. There seems to be the belief, or hope, that somewhere in art we might find a way to dismantle cruelty permanently. In that pursuit, Otomo switches from photography to painting, from the mid-20th-century's demand of the misplaced to Seurat's 1884 vision of urbane harmony, the walk in the park where everyone, even a leashed monkey, fits. She seems to use Seurat simply as her conceptual frame, swerving into a concatenation of odd companions—August Sander, Claude Monet, Caravaggio—but the images these names conjure remain, animating our readings of the poems.

Otomo travels on—poetry her carpet, art her atmosphere. She responds not via criticism but through a personal sense of the value of art and of these particular artists. This sense is tied to an awareness of the fragility of the planet's ecosystem, and art is taken, whatever its vagaries, as a paradigm for vision outside the normal constructive/destructive modes.

Here are some of the guides on her journey:

August Sander.
Josef Beuys.
Marcel Duchamp.
Cornell/Namuth.
Picasso.
Bruce Nauman.
Max Beckmann.
Cy Twombly.
Sarah Sze.
Louise Bourgeois.
Giotto.
Clyfford Still.
Filippino Lippi.
C. D. Friedrich.
Frida Kahlo & Diego Rivera.
Ray Johnson.
Dan Graham.
Mike & Doug Starn.
Suzan Frecon.

Sol LeWitt.

Emma Bee Bernstein.

Barbara Kruger.

Isamu Noguchi.

Odilon Redon.

Philip Guston.

Hannah Wilke & Lona Foote.

I would love to see an exhibition of this grouping Otomo has amassed. I like how her selection puts Sze's work in conjunction with Giotto's and Noguchi's. There is a focus on the eternal qualities of the artists involved, as opposed to their specific, biographical details.

The way nature works in these poems feels ancient. Otomo perceives the spirits in things—in trees, streams, clouds—and remarks on their inhuman abilities. She also blends the human and the non-human, seeing how humans can become attuned to nature's systems:

a boy is born
of a swimmer & a poet

he hears nature's voice
in a perfectly split peach
& he dictates sounds of a brook

(from "Garden [for Isamu Noguchi]")

There is a message here about art and also about man's need to recover his lost tuning.

In her introduction to these poems, Otomo writes of the twin impulses of art and poetry in her own life. Charles Olson wrote, simply and wonderfully: "Art is the only twin life has, its only valid metaphysic." Maybe we could add a corollary: "Art is poetry's twin" (where "art" means "visual art"). Otomo's poems in this volume bring us close to the deep source where poetry and visual art are one. It is not easy to be understanding. Otomo's poetry succeeds and avoids the curse of vituperation.

Vincent Katz

PREFACE

I draw/paint & write. These vocational properties have been with me since I was small. Naturally, painting/drawing surfaced a few years earlier than writing did. Soon after, the skills of reading & writing made available to me the two wheels (or legs) of creativity that carry my being along. Once these two parallel qualities started to germinate within me, my growth has always co-existed with their growth.

I am frequently asked the same two questions: "Which weighs more, visual art or writing?" & "Do you merge the two different worlds/fields? Why or why not?" I usually answer the same way, replying "Neither" to the first question & "No" to the second, with the following reasons why: With my drawing/painting, I search for abstraction. To be as removed from the semantics of language as possible & to learn to assist the self-existence of art within purely visual content—these are among the main purposes of my visual art. I want to see the "invisible" via the act of drawing/painting. As a poet, I belong to the long tradition of the Romantics. I also do some critical writing, in the idiosyncratic mode of an unschooled independent. I get intrigued by my own clearcut & rather abrupt answers to provocative & challenging questions.

Simply stated, these two vocational properties are like "non-identical" twins who do not look alike but who are inseparable, connected on a deep level. They have different faces, voices, temperaments & personalities, but they never step on each other's toes as they move forward together in life; they live in a special kind of empathetic harmony of coexistence. They live side by side inside me without merging or converging with each other. Each sanctuary is for its own sake alone.

However, like life itself or the rules of any game, there are exceptions. The twins meet unexpectedly on some occasions & enjoy playing together as one in the same playground. That's the moment my "art poems" & critical writing come to life. My love & passion for visual art & my inner need to express them come together, as if they are happily holding hands. As I see/observe/appreciate a work of art, my reaction occasionally takes the form of an art poem or of art criticism, crossing the bridge between visual art & writing in the most natural way.

This book collects some of those happy mergings in the form of poems for & about art & artists. I've chosen not to include my critical writings here; art poems & art criticism have different faces, although they share the same instrument/ language. Writing poems on art is like dancing—art puts out a hand (an inspiration) & invites me to move with it. When I do critical writing on art, it is like mountain climbing or deep-sea excavation: I proceed with the process & force my way into finding things out, without an invitation. This book contains only dances.

While gathering materials for STUDY, I noticed two things I hadn't realize before. One is the lack of poems on some of my "favorite" artists (e.g., Matisse; Goya; Pollock...) & an abundance of poems on art I care less personally for. Another peculiar thing is that some art invites me to the poetic world alone, some to the critical world alone & some to both. Bruce Nauman's work more or less rejects my critical abilities, allowing me to write poems instead. Conversely, Matisse

& Pollock elicit only the deep-sea excavation necessary for critical writing, while Louise Bourgeois generously invites me to do both. Through these practices, I've learned one of the most vital truths: "liking" & "disliking" have nothing to do with art.

One of my earliest poems, in Japanese, is called "Resutakku Fukei" (Landscape at L'Estaque). Written for a middle school assigment, it's about a young naïve daydreaming in one of George Braque's pre-Cubist Fauve landscape paintings. The painting was on one of the covers of *Bijutsu Techo*, a Japanese version of *Cahiers d'Art* that my mother occasionally brought home. Since moving to New York City in 1979, I have been blessed by the abundance of "live" art viewing & friendships with artists this city has provided me. The poems included here are the result.

The book consists of two parts. Part I: POEM CYCLES & Part II: ROLLED UP & UNFRAMED/Miscellaneous Poems on Art. Some of the poem cycles were previously published as small-run chapbooks (usually 35–50 copies). Most of the miscellaneous poems are previously unpublished. The majority of the poems here were written in my adopted language, English. Some were composed in Japanese & then later translated into English. Writing in an adopted language is like digesting things with a different DNA filter. Since Japanese allows one to have a much less rigid, almost irrational liberty & abstraction, the strict sense of tense, particles & singularity/plurality that governs English is always a challenge to me. I can't thank steve dalachinsky enough for assisting me through this rather tedious language-adjusting technical process.

The period of writing spans from the early 1980s to the present. The order of the poems in each part is determined by chance operation, disregarding the chronology of creation or the art-historical chronology of artists & their works. I am excited to be giving them a chance to live under one roof.

Yuko Otomo

for steve

if you are Didi, I am your Gogo
if you are Gogo, I am your Didi

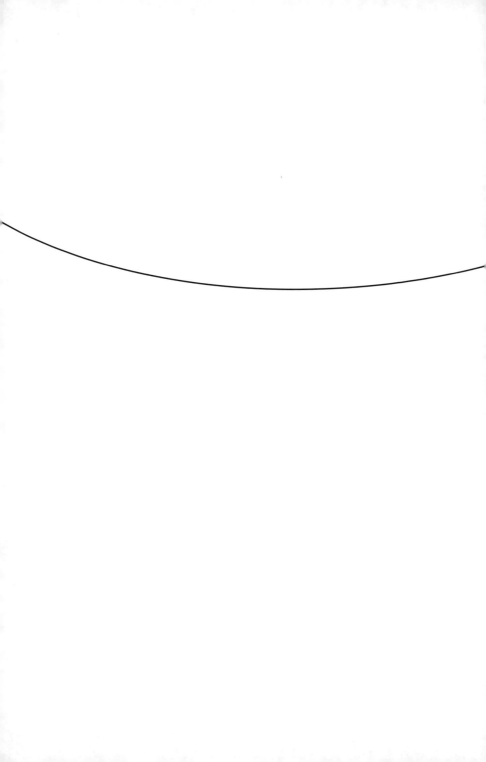

STUDY

STUDY 1: BALANCE & WEIGHT

More
Black on
Black to
Erase the
Center of
(what)?

STUDY 2: SONORITY & RHYTHM

Take
Your
Own
Time
To
Stretch
Out
To
Sing

Louder
&
Livelier

Or

Quieter

STUDY 3: COLOR & COLOR COGNITION PROCESS

Differences
In the two
Are very
Obvious

One is one
Another is another

They both
Are here

STUDY 4: TOOLS & MATERIALS
(for Christine Hughes)

Life is good
Onward & forward

See you very soon
At the same place
At a different date/time

Now I can see
What tools to
Use to get along
With materials

I can dance
With them

STUDY 5: SPACE & BOUNDARY

There is no boundary
In space
But there is

A boundary

In the space
You face

Four corners
Are not the end
But the beginning
Of something bigger

Even deeper

So stop facing
The space

Instead

Become it

STUDY 6: ORDER, CHAOS & MESS

Don't be fetishistic
About order & cleanliness

Get messy
Get dirty

Forget about
Chaos

STUDY 7: SPIRIT & PURPOSE

Don't get meta-physical
When you hold a brush

It teaches you
How to be purposeless
& spiritual

STUDY 8: PRIVATE HISTORY & PUBLIC HISTORY

If you don't say a word
Everybody thinks you are deaf or dumb

But occasionally somebody
In everybody picks the music
In silence

To make your own total

Private history
Of yourself

To be

Shared
By
Others
Besides
You
Alone

STUDY 9: DREAMS & REALITY

No more pressure
To have a layered
Life
Style

Reality
Of
Dream(ing)
Becomes
A dream
Coming
True

STUDY 10: NEW BEGINNING

Just
Begin afresh
Without
Ending
A thing

No more contempt
But
Just
A
Pure
Joy to
Enjoy

—

PART I:

POEM CYCLES

10 POEMS

FOR

"THE AMERICANS"

BY

ROBERT FRANK

PARADE – HOBOKEN, NEW JERSEY

LOVE inside
boxes made of bricks,
lured by the brightness
of a parade passing by,
comes to stand
by the window(frame)s.

LOVE meta-morphed
into different shapes
stands still
by the (window)frames.

Arms of a woman.
Palms of a boy.

An afternoon breeze waves
a flag of IDEALS, DREAMS & the VOID
rectifying HAPPINESS.

As cheers fill the streets,
a new sense of HUNGER
nails the interior darkness down.

FUNERAL – ST. HELENA, SOUTH CAROLINA

We have to wait.
We have to wait,

standing still & patient.

We have to wait.

We press our hands against our lips
& glance at the forest behind,

but hours of the dead
are too remote
for us to reach.

We have to wait.
We have to wait.

Further quieting our breaths down,
we have to wait.

We are allowed to gaze
at a passing shadow of the dead
only briefly

as we rest our cheeks in our hands.

But our departure is still yet forbidden.

We have to wait.
We have to wait.

NEW YORK CITY

A man is a woman
& a woman is a man.

Only when you hide your face,
the world reveals itself
clearly to you.

Human hipbones,
harder than those iron fences,
wind swifter, wiser & faster
than fish bones do.

Troubles; pranks; tricks.

A woman is a man
& a man is a woman
& feet are minds
& eyes are feet.

"Where is today's catch?"

RANCH MARKET – HOLLYWOOD

"Bigger, Better Than Ever!"
"Absolutely No Fillers"
"5 ¢ Extra—"

A waitress's tight red lips
whisper "Merry Christmas"
for all seasons.

YOM KIPPUR – EAST RIVER, NEW YORK CITY

Mist & fog comfort us
as we throw our sins
into the river.

Darkness of our thoughts
is embraced by
our own silence
as it settles down
to be a humble flame.

Father & son
reconcile with
each other
as they float
together
in TIME.

TROLLEY – NEW ORLEANS

It is ME who is looking out
at the passing world,
in a light breeze,
uttering no words to no one,
letting myself rest
on an old wooden bench
of an old trolley
in an old city
where life & death crumble together
in a dark dense humidity.

I am an old woman.
I am a young girl.
I am an old man.
I am a young boy.
I am white.
I am black.
I am rich.
I am poor.

Like framed pictures
of reincarnated multiple lives
I have lived,
liquefied memories of my story
merge into one another
as the old railings sing
an unforgettable melody
of their own history.

ROOMING HOUSE – BUNKER HILL, LOS ANGELES

It is a play.
I am an actor.
I am on a stage.
I am costumed, as directed,
in a dark suit with a hat & a cane.

I say nothing,
hiding partially
under the weathered wooden staircase.

A curtain is up
with the late afternoon air
as its only audience.

A room is free & empty.

The season is unknown.

I stay motionless
till the air flow changes
to shift the angle
of light/darkness
of the day.

VIEW FROM HOTEL WINDOW – BUTTE, MONTANA

I was here once.
Who was I with?
I have no recollection.
But, I remember
how my heart ached when I saw
the devastation of human lives
& its resulting landscape
outside my hotel window.

Was I with a man? Or was I with a woman?
Was I with a friend? Or was I with a lover?
I have no memory.
But, I can never forget
the way my soul trembled
when I breathed in the gray silence
of the flat roofs & cruel, clumsy insignificant chimneys.
I don't remember what day it was,
but I remember that
I was shattered totally
by the fragile beauty of the fluttering curtains
that divided my room
from the view outside.

"People live here."
I remember muttering
to the one next to me.

I don't remember who it was,
but I remember that
we were once definitely
here together.

U.S. 285, NEW MEXICO

Space rejects names.
Space is limitless.
Space disappears in itself,
creating a mirage
of Horizon.

Day is long.
Night is dark.
Road is piercingly indifferent
to everyone & everything.

When it disappears
into Horizon,
it crosses
itself.

BAR – NEW YORK CITY

Don't shout!
Speak easy in a hush!
A jukebox, shining like a monolith,
serenades a popular song
of our youth.

Let's fool ourselves thinking
it's not drinks that we want,
but the shaded interior
of "somewhere" where
the sun doesn't reveal
the details of our lives
too cruelly.

Let's speak in a dry whisper,
pretending that the sticky floors & a cloudy mirror
suit our desire well to be left alone.

Let's act as if we were proud & civil,
not sullen & disproportioned.

Let's enjoy the dark daydreaming
together believing that
everything is fine & dandy

finally.

from A SUNDAY AFTERNOON ON THE ISLE OF MUSEUM

(after Seurat's "A Sunday Afternoon on the Island
of La Grand Jatte")

AUGUST

a)

Another August
another summer
(passing).

A coal heaver,
a student of philosophy,
a painter's daughter,
road construction workers
or even a pharmacist,

people

without failing
never change.

They stare back
at the impersonal demand
of the camera's eye.

Rich with visions & tastes,
supported by their sturdy postures
& well-woven fabrics,
farmers stand firmly
in their focused self-reliance.

b) Work Types – physical & intellectual

Shipyard workers
& carpenters
look less dishevelled
& tortured than
a trio of revolutionaries.

County workers
& a communist leader,
they both look like
schoolmasters
with a hidden trait
of oppressed sexuality.

Dark, stern & direct,
a painter's eyes
do not wait
for a "go"
from a cameraman.

Drunk
in the realm
of structural tonality
& mathematics,
composers proudly
but sadly
sit alone.

Living in a celluloid mirror,
a moving wagon
or on a gilded stage,

actors, male or female,
know how to stare
into the void.

Naturally, businessmen & politicians
hide the most & the worst of themselves
under their well-tailored coats.

A secretary at the radio station
in the 1930s is called
a woman of intellectual & practical occupation.
She sits in the most stable manner
looking erotically androgynous.

An aristocrat
sneaks his glances
like an arrogant
but meek rat.
He looks the stupidest.

Clergymen
are uncertain
of the points
where they stand.

Gypsies & transients,
I feel personally
the closest to these travelling people
& their open & dead-end melancholy.

The persecuted;
a look of professorship
unnoticed.

A blind miner & a blind soldier
dig ditches together in timelessness.

Idiots, the sick, the insane
& matter,
they are always treated
as one bunch.

A death mask
of a son of a son
of a carpenter
takes the longest breath
looking thousands of years old.

Leaving all these variations
on the same thematic portraits
of people of the (20th) Century,
an old farmer walks
into dusk kinetically
with 2 canes
supporting his 2 legs.
He looks back at us
unknowingly.

REST: MONET ROOM

a) water lilies

I am not tired
but I take a rest
in your garden full
of memories of
exposed negatives
& dark water.

Sky/clouds are the best thing
of the day.

Always.

Always.

As a poet sings
in every century.

b) sunflowers & chrysanthemums

I am not tired
but I take a rest
among the crowd
for a while.

Women in floral patterns
come in & out of my sight.

Women, we are lucky
for not having to go through
psychological complications
when we wrap ourselves
in flowers & colors.

c) Komore-bi/Nature Morte

Still life: apples & grapes
on your table
repeatedly tell
the untold story
of your daily routines.

PAINTERS OF REALITY

a)

Sleep walking
in the dream reality,
I bump into
another reality
avoiding the other.

Marble floors
& gray-beige walls
corner our unconcerned
sense of beauty.

A head on a plate.
A skull in an open hand.

I rejoice
an unexpected reunion
with a girl
whom I met
for the first time
when she was 10 days old.

The idea of naturalism,
to observe nature,
can always be retained & reassured
in your most personal reality.

b)

Fidelity to truth,   il vero.
Emotions,   affetti.
Motions of the mind,   moti mentali.

Blackberries.
Cranberries.

In every century,
in every region,

a man & a woman
do their best to
perfect their skill
of burying themselves impersonally
in a humble, but a dramatic
juicy climax
of the season.

So do artists
when they study
a delicate botany anatomy.

c) Bergamo: Devotional Art

A man carries a cross
among the crowd.

We hear no roars, no howls, no chatters
in this muted & resigned
disconsolateness.

d) shepherd with a flute

I sit down among the crowd
to let myself secretly be drawn
to the dark blue shade
of your gaze under the wide brimmed hat.

An intense sky
around you
intensifies its intensity itself
more & more,
it turns itself
into a glass-like
transparency
of hard liquidity.

You, alone, sit there,
holding a flute in your hands.

Such a beautiful face,
such a gentle slope
of your shoulders & arms!
& such clean sturdy
working hands & fingers!

In your posing posture,
silence is music,
a melody that never reaches
anyone, anywhere.

As clouds form
ungraspable poetry of the day,

so high up in the sky
making human thoughts
immensely dark,
red sleeves sing
your masculine elegance
in a pure pre-operatic
canto.

e) Caravaggio (Michelangelo Merisi)

A young man
playing a concerto,
a lute player,
flowers,
an open score
& instruments.

It's a shame
that I have to share
you with hundreds
of others.

In your eyes,
exterior & interior
of every organism
manifest their realities
in such a clean undaunted conviction.

Your grapes, your angel glance,
your robes, your young boys' skin
& their gaze.

What is hidden
& what is exposed,
all float out
in the form
of a small breath of Eros
between 2 slightly
untouched lips.

Light & shadow
never sing
different songs
nor play unrelated notes.

In your room,
dense with
sacred secular
concentration,
I lose
my ability
to poeticize
things.

f) Unframed St. Matthew and the Angel

Witnessing
numerous nails
& 400 years or more old
woven fiber
leaves me
completely
speechless.

The crowd
weaves through
the space around me
in a casual humbleness.

A girl walks
in front of me
to face the mysterious meeting
of an old vulgar man-saint
& a young man-angel.

She breaks
her own & my
concentration,
sneezing.

In this cloudless space,
we all, one way or another,
wrap ourselves
in aesthetic details
of woven cotton fabrics.

Secular
or sacred,
metamorphosis
of a material reality
still amazes me.

g) still life

> What we eat.
> What we grow.
> What we collect.
> What we harvest.
> What we decorate.
> What we put into a bowl,
> on a plate or in a basket.

> An illusion
> of Nature Morte
> betrays itself
> vividly & vengefully
> to claim its life
> at the moment.

h) The Supper at Emmaus: Tremendous Naturalezza (Tremendous Naturalism)

> After the resurrection,
> he casts a shadow
> in light.

> The room
> is dark
> with a gray cloudy floor.

> I see a cornered void
> of the scene
> together

in amazement
with 3 protagonists.

A basket of fruits
meat on a plate,
bread, wine & water,
solid & unshakable,
evidence of this
tremendous reality
tells the story
of resurrected flesh.

What words
are breathing out
from your closed mouth?

Acclaiming his faith
in the ability
to express
the reality around him
without stylistic structures,
an artist
wakes up
to another reality
shot suddenly
by a dart of a closing call
coming from
nowhere.

ARENA

a linked poem collaboration with steve dalachinsky
on Joseph Beuys' work with the same title, 1992

sd: steve dalachinsky
yo: Yuko Otomo

sd   the meat is dead the bones of the architect reconstruct

yo   the sun or a circle on my back to scratch

sd   waxen I am shot with fingers raised in safety

yo   my palm aims at a bullet

sd   a patch un-patch

yo   re-joy(ce)? they've never taught me how to be joyous

sd   no answer no choice, I call & repeat like a reel, Ulysses

yo   a lined-up ever-ness & its skeleton

sd   effervesces in a pile of shit & 2 fingers point from dead skin

yo   I want to hear & see who's behind the wall

sd   wired to gumshoe

yo   is it morning or night? the time is shown with hands
        pointing at 2

sd   lard & sharp nail retract

yo   I tried to sew a shell with no thread
        & to cook my mind in a small pot

sd   the secret of us like wire in the dead mouse palm
yo   I am asked to sit down on a wooden stool

in front of a wooden desk to look at a wooden board
your hand is too clean to show me anything

sd   I am the black cross survive & fight with sturdy back bone

yo   even the artist is allowed to be happy & shy sometimes

sd   toast & waffle the music is silent & rapt
I drill holes in a body silenced & wrapped
I lie down & my mouth becomes the floor

yo   I was born out of those huge rags, someone told me

sd   the blue & yellow of a blizzard
the brown hammer
the form of snow on a pyramid
a steel door or a pelvis

yo   wire-inscribed history

sd   I go through hoops
I accuse you in harsh light, in black square, you who gag
the piano

yo   please ask me a question when you know the answer!
to sweep the floor is more important for me at this moment

sd   my ear becomes the sand, the dust, the stone

yo   magnified dirt, a perfect square, a perfect shadow, a
perfect corner—
when a man plays a violin, we see a mist(fog)

sd   white cross my face becomes the muffler
           my word first muffed, then mute

yo   sitting, listening to my knees, I take my temperature
           when I wake up, I'll surely eat my pillow
           "why is he wearing a fur coat in the forest anyway?"

sd   dead fish & relic, loose hair & dancing girls
           naked women drawn

yo   I dream & play a felt-covered piano
           it is going to be a slow & sad, mean song
           + & − lie on their stomachs

sd   a light attached

yo   a perfect triangle, a perfect hat
           I make a speech to a woman
           when a horse feeds itself nights & days

sd   the soles of my feet alone

yo   a fish stuck with positives moves quickly
           to light bulbs, to the dead mouse

sd   a light attached to my arse, black cross again
           but now on keys, no longer in tune with your name

yo   please do not write anything on the blackboard
           I do not have to learn anything

sd   you hang like a rag with brother's death mask on your face
           & the image in the negative of your shirt

yo   we shoot rabbits/hares, don't we?

sd   rolled like a rug, the record plays only the scratches

yo   a blue panel, another blue panel & then a yellow panel

sd   fish trawl & your lips the same & eyes as dark as a well

yo   arena of Verona to see the mountains far

sd   the words are not important said the old woman
        reading

yo   a horse & my shirt share the color

sd   a torah disarmed & desiccated, a midget kills the beast
        grease shocking Verona men

yo   a perfect corner, a perfect room, an imperfect fuss

sd   you listen to air through copper tube & wax—

yo   I see the heart beat of the air
        a perfect loop, a perfect malice, a perfect dust

sd   the wildlife on stilts is frozen by removing its innards

yo   I am crossed with an triangle & my bones ache
        to be with time is tearing me part

sd   element 1, element 2,
        I'll draw you an unreadable diagram
        & pull rabbits from my hat, my coat, my glove

yo   a perfect dance, a perfect collusion

sd   I like my cheek on night pillow & my architect bones
reunite

yo   I sit on my knees, on water, to learn to be a quiet
alchemist—
I do not need a mirror anymore

sd   the cymbals crack, I bury my secrets in the corner

yo   fat & snow share the same color

sd   cold shock one spin left on the old wood chair

yo   I have to bend my back to touch the floor

sd   bent at the knees, a swarm of darkness warns me

yo   a hand to direct nothing

sd   in the broken mirror detached from machine
black cross again

yo   a box to hold nothing

sd   piles of whys rolled us on sleds, we bathe in tracks

yo   a man's face that does not talk—
silence is his words

sd   like an almost empty box
I feed on you-as-king

yo   please do not tell me to climb up
           I've never even been at the bottom of the sea

sd   the brain drawn & heavy like snow

yo   a corrosion wrapped with a thin net

sd   I hang like a hand like a hanger on a hand on a nail
           on a cross where I hang

yo   a perfect bath tub, a perfect profile

sd   I drop it

yo   lined-up watches show different time

sd   the arena is empty except your horse
           your outstretched arms, your imprisoned white horse

yo   a book is open

4 FOR MARCEL DUCHAMP

MARCEL DUCHAMP

he was
a dandy

he was
a cigar-smoking
gentle-man

DUCHAMPIAN RECONSTRUCTION OF MY PERSONALITY

learn to be idle
& not to feel guilty
about it

MY GUESS OF MARCEL DUCHAMP'S FAVORITE WORD

fine

SOME PRACTICAL LESSONS TO LEARN TO BE A GRANDDAUGHTER OF MARCEL DUCHAMP

speak less
or talk less
(to say more)
or
talk less
(to say less)

let the rest rest

be a verb

be idle & (be) guiltless
be idle & (be) joyful
be idle & (be) good
be idle

be free

be free & be nothing

be nothing

it's not important
to be nothing

take a walk
or
stroll

run if you like

from CORNELL BOX POEMS

PART I
Hans Namuth's Photography of Joseph Cornell

PART II
Cornell Boxes & Collages

PART I

JOSEPH CORNELL IN HIS GARDEN   (HANS NAMUTH 1969)

a neighbor raises
her voice in a hush
"the weather is changing—"
she detects the mood of the air
through the glass window
of her second floor room

uncountable wash lines,
mostly empty

a man is a man, a mother, a brother
he quietly closes himself
to be open
to a dream of birds & stars
a man, a martyr & a shell
sits alone
in a green flooding garden

soon, we will witness an empty chair—
woodenness of it will be clear,
then

STUDIO DETAILS OF STORAGE RACKS   (HANS NAMUTH 1973)

shells, sea shells, plastic shells, 1969.
stamps, sand, bottles, biscuits de lux cherrydale farm.
tin cans, penny arcade, boxes/empty.
deep seas, nights, days, mid days.

best white boxes, cotton, shadows, rings.
love letters to jennifer jones.
love letters to jennifer jones.
snow flakes, birds, nests, feathers.

CORNELL HOUSE AT 37-07 UTOPIA PARKWAY   (HANS NAMUTH 1973)

it is a clear crisp suburban christmas
no one is allowed to open
the windows from outside

STUDIO, DETAILS OF WORK BENCH   (HANS NAMUTH 1973)

an american train is passing
a wind mill, smoking

in woods, birds listen to its sounds
coming closer & closer

they sweetly face the direction of night
resting their feathers & feet
on fragile rims of clear glass jars—
when day takes the stage over
they change themselves into
a tight-mouthed ancient-faced girl

she stares at an atlas
in her hand, an hour glass of eternity
as light veils dust

mist—
roundness—
flatness—
many faded colors to come & go—

an artist finally
touches eros & thanatos
at random

CORNELL'S BASEMENT STUDIO   (HANS NAMUTH 1969)

1.
   sphinx is tilted
   head down
   but no one thinks of the danger
   of it falling—
   "it is floating, rather,"

   cartoonish existence of an ajax box
   is mute, sedate, humble & decent
   in this brick constructed space

   tea & coffee travel
   across the ocean
   in a package labeled
   "delicacies"

who would even doubt
the weightless weight of a feather's shadow
when beethoven's sonata seduces
the bitter sweet memory
of an empty french chocolate box?

2.

a small box
tied up forever
with thin strings
does not ask anyone
to let it open

no reason discussed

art lies down
on a corner table
mutely in dust
sometimes it answers a call from bellow
other times it answers a call from above

PART II

CORNELL BOX #1: UNTITLED   (HOTEL DES VOYAGEURS)

"please do not trap me in eternity!"

I am afraid, trembling,
walking on the thin rim of a white porcelain universe
I am praying, saying,

"please do not let me fall!"

before my eyes, blue seas
behind my eyes, sunset
below & above me is a dark tender eternity

I am an euphoria
tight-roping on memory & myth
I am an acrobat
who never learns how to make a balance

"Apollinaire!"

this will be my first scream
if I ever fall

"Apollinaire!"

this will be my last scream
if I ever fly away

"Apollinaire!"

& then, soon,

I will find myself
sweetly sleeping
in a lovely room
in Hotel des Voyageurs

dreaming
nothing

CORNELL BOX #2: UNTITLED   (LA BELLA)

sternly opened eyes can see
anything they want—

female softness is a vice
someone said

but beauty is always a dream-like child
not to know where to go

CORNELL BOX #3: SOAP BUBBLE SET

when I was a very young girl
I used to admire a man's profile
especially if he had a moustache
just like the one you see
in the picture book on 19th Century history

& I wish I was a man
forgetting that
I was born to be a woman

red,
yellow,
green,

& blue lightness of light

CORNELL BOX #5: CELESTIAL NAVIGATION BY BIRDS

a girl touches a crystal glass
softly & tenderly
with her small finger tips

birds
waking up from an eternal sleep
fly away

sounds of their navigating wings
make the shape of a sea shell
washed ashore to linger on
in her dreamy eyes

CORNELL BOX #6: UNTITLED   (PARROT & BUTTERFLY HABITAT)

a conversation
an argument
an exchange of words
a competition

"what noisy creatures they are! they can't stop talking!"
"what busy creatures they are! they can't stop flapping their wings!"

"what a fate to share space with them!"
"what a fate to share space with them!"

"no wonder the artist wanted to have a netted fence between us!"
"no wonder the artist wanted to have a netted fence between us!"

thinking separately in their own languages
they both thank Mr. Cornell for having such a kind &
        thoughtful idea

paper parrots, paper butterflies
they are too proud to be nice to each other
but, funny,
they are equally proud of their beautiful coloring

CORNELL BOX #7: OBJECT   (HOTEL THEATRICALS)
a 4-act play played mischievously by marbles, red, green & blue

ACT 1: The Triumph of Galatia

Pygmalion thought he won
when Aphrodite granted his prayer
& danced in joy
but, the truth is that–
the nothing & everything-ness of beauty determined
its own fate
over the hard-minded goddess
& the self-feeding creator

ACT 2: The Finding of Moses in the Bulrushes

two hands to shed blood
two hands to give mercy
oh, poor soul
you escaped death
but you had to suffer
the refusing coldness of the wetlands
for such a long time

ACT 3: The Visit of the Queen of Sheba to Solomon

when the Queen of Sheba visited him
King Solomon had gone through enough extravagances
a so-called sexual attraction seemed too mundane
for his well fed taste
but the smell of spices she carried around
made him almost blind
& her sweet eagerness to learn wisdom
utterly impressed him

ACT 4: Jacob Wrestles with the Angel

a little girl in the audience
is wondering
how the angel's wings would taste
if she bites into them
an old man in the audience
is remembering
his first love

CORNELL BOX #12: UNTITLED   (DOVECOTE-AMERICAN)

1.

where are they,
birds of latitude?
are they gone or
are they sleeping in their dream?

here in America
every second is day & night

where are they,
birds of longitude?
have they flown away or
are they dreaming in their sleep?

here in America
every season is summer & winter

2.

fama sollicitus–
imo adoratio–
gentis More's–
forsan est–

a four-cornered history of ingrained ideals
sing busy songs
silently
in an empty white nest

3.

    doves are sleeping
    someone is reading a newspaper
    in a foreign tongue loudly

    "Today No War Breaks Out!"

CORNELL BOX #13: IMAGES FOR 2 EMILIES

Emily was blue
before she was born

Emily will be blue
after she stops being Emily

a tear drops
when something happy happens

a tear drops
when something sad happens

when TIME throws its thorny title away
Emily faces herself

doubling her images on tears
politely set in small necked glasses

alone she nods sweetly
to affirm her good manner & etiquette

CORNELL BOX #14: PANTRY BALLET   (FOR JACQUES OFFENBACH)

zag zag zag zag
zug zug zug zug
zag zag zag zag
zag zag zag zag
tin tin tin tin
la la la la
rattle rattle rattle rattle
crank crank crank crank
chuck chuck chuck chuck
roop roop roop roop
op op op op
knock knock knock knock
tap tap tap tap

look look look look

how we dance

CORNELL COLLAGE #17: INTERPLANETARY NAVIGATION

born
to be as sweet as
2 flying birds

(aren't we?)

born
to be as modest as
early morning clouds

(aren't we?)

we play a clarinet
sleeping
waking
we see ourselves
navigating
from one sphere to another

(don't we?)

is it a dream?

(isn't it?)

shall we sing?
or shall we cry?

born
to be as light as
feathers' shadows

(aren't we?)

born
to be as quiet as
smooth surfaced marbles

(aren't we?)

PICASSO MUSEUM

PICASSO MUSEUM

I.

Incandescent empathy,
becoming one with passion,
gazed into blueness
of the world.

Languidly curved laboring arms.
A head of a woman resting in a palm.
A drooping mystery.

Dry blood of Spain
helped to taint
the world he is gazing at
further deeply blue.

II.

To be a clown.
To induce laughter out of other(s).
To fetch a pump to call for
"Joy of Life."

Walking across the spherical world,
verifying its vastness under their minute feet,
a Human Family shines
in rose colors.

III.

An artist's mind/heart
responded warmly
to various vicissitudes
of the Human World
in rose colors.

IV.

Standing figures of women
were so overtly
clean & violent that
he stumbled.

Eternity sees all
in its earthly agitation.

Women's glances
into the air
were so overtly
cunning & placid that
he took up his paint brushes.

Eternity knows all
in its earthly delight.

V.

Things break up into pieces.
Light & shadow join their company.

Here.

An apple's sweetness
never gets called into question.
A pear's form terminates.

VI.
Things fall into pieces.
Light & shadow escape from their world.

An apple's sweetness
is now a thing of the past.
A pear's form is
reborn as Essence

for the first time.

VII.
A large majority of people
incurred suspicions
over his passion.

He made a guitar
a tool to compensate
his mind/heart.

VIII.
Letters & numbers.
& their peculiar sense of Modernity.

& his peculiar participation
to their peculiar world.

IX.

A man who could not
give up his longing
for ancient times
started to glorify
the flesh = body.

Again.

A man who could not
fully be aware of
living in the present
gave a dream back
to the figures of
a mother & a child.

Again.

X.

A woman who cries.
A woman who gets startled
by her own image in a mirror.
A woman who stimulates an artist
& his simple consciousness
just by lying down in front of him.

Human Thoughts
grandly occupy
the Human World.

XI.

A sense of the direction of severity.

XII.

Stop looking
for a symbol
in an ox's horns.

A cat with prey
smacks his lips
brightly.

XIII.

Longing for Nostalgia
in a woman's body,
a man copulates with
a woman.

Feeling victorious
for being desired,
a woman returns Love to
a man.

The artist concluded
that a carnal interchange
induces the one with the soul
as well

after all.

XIV.

Antipathy toward atrocity
occupied an artist's mind/heart.

He dashes into the depth of Darkness
after hearing the voice of Justice
in the world of Night.

Seeing Void
in his self-portrait,
an artist realizes
that a cycle has been completed.

FRAGILE

a poem cycle for the work of Bruce Nauman

A plea by a crazed orator with a harmonica in his hands

reality
is a food
when you take a bite
outs of it
you will faint

(a found poem on the subway platform at 53rd St. & 5th Ave.
on 4.4.1995, the day I saw the Nauman retrospective at
MoMA, NYC)

FALL   (FOR B. N.)

1.
a man walks
he falls
first
on his knees
palms
then on his elbows & cheeks
& finally on his belly

the waving horizon
is very clear
& he likes it

think me
make me
ache me
wake me

lying flat
he is somehow comfortable
with his new luxury

a woman sits
on a chair
hanging upside down
in the air
so naturally
she falls
& the chair follows
together

they fall into
nowhere in particular

take me
think me
rake me
ache me

floating
she is somehow happy
with her new formality

2.

we make magic, shadow plays, even language
with our hands

what expressive golden tools we are given!

a king, a queen, bishops & knights
have been dead for a long time
but they still play hide & seek
through the faces of playing cards

finally,
we have begun to realize the non-sense-ness
of the purpose of this game

3.
AH, HA

life & death

a triple-pianissimo-earth
a war-earth

eat shit & die
pay attention, mother-fuckers!

mirrored images of logos
buried with messages
jump at us & bark at
our overly self-conscious nerves
whenever we imagine
we are walking
into a forest of con-science

PARALLELOGRAM   (1971)

you walk in
not just to stand in the room
but to see something

an empty weight crashes down on you
& you yourself become an empty space
you soon realize that
an aim or your eagerness
to want to see things
makes no sense at all

Philips screws, compressed sheet rock walls
disconnect time from time

open palms call you to look at them—

there, you see a map of blood
marbling into something
you have never seen before

CORRIDOR INSTALLATION (NICK WILDER INSTALLATION)

1.
it is me
who is walking
in a corridor

I see my out-lined image/shadow
at the dead end
& it looks almost monstrous

I don't see my
face, nor eyes
not even my skin nor hair color

white-irradiating walls
are like an air
full of denials

the light goes off
when I become conscious
of my (own) back

2.
I walk
in a corridor

& sink into the ocean
where I am bound
to be cradled & rocked

this way & that
by a slow metronome rhythm

I don't care to see
my image in this wide-enough-space

3.

I stand vertically
you stand horizontally
& we look at each other
& don't notice
where the floor & ceiling
become one to satisfy our curiosity

SLOW ANGLE WALK/BECKETT WALK   (1968)

it is dramatic
how I've finally
come to the realization
that I walk
on 2 feet

I can't
stop looking at
my toes
whenever I
step
ahead

RAW WAR   (1970)

RAW WAR WAR
RAW WAR WAR
RAW WAR WAR
RAW WAR WAR

3 red letters
bark at you
in 3 balanced
raw voices

YELLOW ROOM (TRIANGULAR)   (1973)

a straight line
warps itself
so hard
trying to
touch my
surface = skin

2 people
meet for the 1st time
& they
smile at
each other

BANG!

the end

MUSICAL CHAIRS: STUDIO VERSION   (1980)

I don't hear
anything not even
a voice going
up & down the scales

hanging on the equator

I suddenly remember
my parents & their
occupations

VIDEO

in the room
with a (tv) monitor
a pair of speakers
& a dozen chairs
with no audience
except myself

the screen keeps telling me
"it's video 3," "it's video 3," "it's video 3"
but never opens
a door for me

100 LIVE AND DIE   (1984)

Kiss and Live
Stand and Live
Live and Die
Eat and Die
Touch and Live

Life shines
in Technicolor
Death shines
in Technicolor

until we really learn
how to

Fall and Live

VIOLENT INCIDENT   (1986)

a daily diet
of courtesy & decency
depends too much
on every passing second of
our precious time

for nothing

on the table in the midst of
a violent incident

flowers in a vase
remain flowers

UNTITLED   (TWO WOLVES, TWO DEER)

a disgust
stills
a windmill
when silence
occupies
our bellies

my fear
is glued
to a wire
so nothing will ever
escape my cross

CLOWN TORTURE   (1987)

finally I am in the room where Micah stayed mesmerized for
more than 45 minutes. funny! I've never really given a thought
to the life of a clown! the life of a clown! the destiny to be a
clown! wow! this clown is not blue, he is red! he is standing
talking in a horizontal position. I don't know what he's saying,
but I see his mean-looking mouth move non-stop. definitely
he's saying something, clinging to a stiff broom hanging from
the ceiling. is he complaining or is he pleading? wait a minute!

I think I can hear what the clown is saying now. it sounds like he is confessing some personal matter. it almost sounds like he's saying something like "is it my fate or my free will that has made me a clown? to be honest, I don't mind being a clown. I don't mind being tortured either. because when I'm tortured I can shout 'NO! NO! NO!' out loud without feeling remorse or self-conscious guilt. the more I say 'NO! NO! NO!' the happier people become. I am a happy clown because I am well loved and well rewarded every moment of this GODDAMMED life...etc...etc..." it is strange and scary to listen to a clown talk like this... I don't think I'd enjoy the life of a clown myself. it is too raw for me. something is too sticky about the life of a clown. I'd rather shout "YES! YES! YES!" though it means all the same.

TEN HEADS CIRCLE/UP AND DOWN   (1990)

before I pull my tongue in again
I know I will melt into the air

remember, I have no spine of thoughts
when I stand on your resigned head(s)

SHIT IN YOUR HAT – HEAD ON A CHAIR   (1990)

mimicking what you do helplessly
according to my ideology
guided by a tri-colored traffic light

I regret to obey your order
I used to have nose bleed as a child
so I share precisely the feeling
of a nose being stuffed with foreign matter

I have never had
my own room, my own chair, so as a result
I have no place to rest my summer hat safely

you'll have to excuse me
when I say "no" to your request
to show you my hat at season's end

hanging stiffly, loose in the air,
I am still wondering
if you share my feelings
as much as I share yours

POKE IN THE EYE/NOSE/EAR (3/8/94 EDIT)   (1994)

Spain is far-away
although
books on Picasso
fill my shelves

some very watery substance
pisses out
whenever I
think of squeezing
my psyche

so, instead

I poke my eyes,
nose, ear
in such
slow motion
that no body
will ever catch
up to me
when I
need to run
away

WORLD PEACE   (1996)

our faces
our hair
our voices
our need
to talk whatever
to whomever listens

no matter what

disgust
me

I am completely fed up
with my self-consciousness
witnessing

7 holes in our heads confessing
a trite trieste of our existence

wet or dry
I'll never listen

you'll talk to me
I'll never listen to you

END OF THE WORLD I   (1996)

I never get impressed
when someone says or sings the promise
"I'll love you till the end of the world"

I was born awake

the world ended
when I was thrown into it

END OF THE WORLD II

1. I have thought of the end of the world many times,
    audio-visualizing its scenery & its sounds.
    how does the wind blow in such a situation?

2. thanks for letting me know that the breeze will breeze
    through us

at the end of the world where a comforting light will
congratulate us
for being able to fulfill our long wished goal perfectly.

3.   blue gray, turning into almost blue purple—
slant your eyes a bit to the opposite side,
you will see the color change.

red red,
red red,
the sun rises & sets
even when nobody sees it.

with or without the voice that says "who cares!?!"
the breeze will breeze
through the pale green emptiness.

wavelets of the prevailing oceans will move more
delicately & seductively.

they will even sing songs for us
who are not there any more.

shading blue.
fading blue.
rainbow blue.
rainbow blue purple.

the breeze will breeze through itself
at the end of the world

with no one to give hands for the climactic spectacle.
no one taps toes, no one relaxes in (his/her) shoes.

nothing gained.
nothing lost.

the breeze will talk to the void in its own landscape.
the breeze will breeze through itself.

through itself through itself through itself.

through itself through itself.

through & through...................

HANDS UNTITLED   (AFTER B. N.'S UNTITLED WHITE BRONZE LIFE SIZE HANDS ON METAL BASE, 1996)

I am standing
in bright light
contemplating
on the way
a hand holding a hand
so they do not get drowned
in a bliss

male
female
female
male
male

they are all united

nails to nails
skin to skin
a palm to a palm
hands
climb & crumble
on a cliff

of emotional lives
but they never get used to thrills
adventures provide

a sphere
a lake
a ladder
a collision
a copulation
a puzzle
a testing trick
a dance, of course
a joke, again, of course
a coquetry
a deceit
a sign

we do things
we make things
with hands untitled
a back to a back
five fingers to five fingers
locked
loosened
& eternally trapped
in the shapes they create

we float
we see
we suggest
with hands
mostly empty

awake

or

not

FRAGILE   (AFTER MAPPING THE STUDIO II WITH COLOR SHIFT, FLIP, FLOP & FLIPFLOP – "FAT CHANCE JOHN CAGE," 2001)

sleeping,
I try to describe
the faces of Time.

pretending
to stand
in the midst
of a housed silence

in the night field,

I let myself be amused,
talking
to cups/hats/chairs/nails
in borrowed words.
breaking the framed monotony
of circumstances,

I circle my own scope around myself
a bit off-balanced.

mice come in & out
in a flash
as a cosmology
based on the floor map
gives a delectation
to dust.

finally,

a slower than usual
howl(ing) of darkness
permits
a physicist's awareness
of dimensions
a little more acceptable
to the general mass.

GENESIS

Max Beckmann Poems

JOURNEY ON THE FISH (MAN AND WOMAN)

we are tied
together
by an eternal fate

I, holding your darkened mask,
you, mine

your silenced flesh
becomes mine
when I bury my face
into the palm of the sea

MORALS

with his hollowed eyes stuffed
by a vortex of seer's contradictions
he is determined to try to pierce the darkness of his times

contemplating ideas of race & species
a man, (un)knowingly pushes
his elbows against the picture frame
which is set to secure his position & status

feet bleeding
he acts the fatal role of Christ
just to return to the original sight
of a passion play

on a barren hill
he sees nothing
but a vast melancholic void
shared by both tortures & sweet prayers

"Oh, Eros! Oh, Lord!"

he shouts
his last words

TREES & HOUSES

a balloon,
an umbrella,
a lamp post,
none of them
argues with the sky
where weightlessness is
always ready to morph itself
on anyone's request
for any possible idiom & identity

GENESIS

he & she stood
by a slow blooming yellow iris
for the first time together

the earth was insistently naïve,
simply flat & round,
under their feet

since words
such as *"pessimism"* or *"optimism"*
were not yet invented,

they had no reason
to pay attention to the call of evil
disguised as a snake

for the same reason,
they had no way of anticipating
a passion play: the mockery of a burning heart

they were just born

they had no need of discussing
"what is pure" & *"what is not"*

IDEOLOGY OF HELL

no one cries
but screams, sobs & moans
in Hell

forced to carry a cross & gun powder on his shoulders
the one who breathes thick faultless air
becomes instantaneously patriotic

& praises the various intentions
of socio-political metaphysics
invented by picnickers

IDEOLOGY OF HEAVEN

sunflowers & chimneys
share the same afternoon shade

electric lines
run through the sky
pretending to create
a clean image
of an unused music sheet

a dog sleeps,
content,
in an empty lot
in Frankfurt

35/35

hands to grasp
every raw element
of the picture book perfection
of being (hu)man

reoccurring dreams
to examine
thin ironies
our piety has created

shoe laces
to tie

numbers to
count

& then deny
later

FEMALE DANCER

as she performs
a Russian split,
her soft-hard spine
curves naturally in a right angle

religious emotions
are nothing but a desperate yearning
to touch
anything that reflects
a perfectly balanced form,
a body myth

ACTOR

wearing a costume of blue/gray,
I throw myself thoroughly
toward an exotic desire
to swim against the stream
in front of the crowd
just to show them
that my poor vocabulary to deliver
what's on my mind
has nothing to do
with the intense silence
I am enveloped in

I fish by the lake
I hunt in the woods
I mine in the quarry
like two fallen candles,
I rest my legs down in bed
by the red curtain at night

interrupted by the crowd's eager appetite for disguises,
I often walk away
from the familiar stage swiftly & proudly
as I give them back
the first line I ever learned to memorize,

"I am not a still life"

BIRTH

when hot water
was poured
into the moment of day break
I, a new born, tragically
fell into night

DEATH

hanging upside down
in the fragile architecture of Time
I long to make love to a fish

.   .   .

in light,
scents of flowers & voices of the choir in ritual costumes
peacefully ripple a similar sense of anonymity
manifested by the modest & cruel horror of our species

.   .   .

a woman
contemplates
the glow
of a new born
she has just delivered

VEGETABLE

names of vegetables
are much easier

to remember
than those of fish

THE PRODIGAL SON: A GAME OF TITLING WORK

among swine
among courtesans
feasting on
disillusionment
together
with beggars

the chimney sweep
never makes up his mind over
what to sing
when drunk

all he cares about
is to drink up what he has
fall asleep soundly
& dream of resurrection
which hopefully takes place
in some flower-blooming season

ALLEGORICAL MORALS

caged,
we discuss
our sense of guilt
over history

rarely
does an artist
paint our sphere
as it is

in fragile air
between the end of one bridge
& the beginning of another,
we dream-walk armored
by our allegorical senses of morals
& the vivid images
of our earlier selves

IN GRAY

we gradually lose ourselves
in our own footsteps
as we get closer
to the mountain top

my wife in gray,
I in blue/black,
we keep talking of the image

of the run down station we passed
on some rainy afternoon

"When we reach the top,
Where can we go?" she asks half-jokingly

forced to be orphans in eternity,
just to break the monotony of our daily routines,
we switch roles & costumes
occasionally

ANATOMY OF MELANCHOLY

after Cy Twombly's "Untitled"

ANATOMY OF MELANCHOLY I

spraying water all over silence
I sit in history's grainy shadows

waves weighed lead-heavy with silver lights
crash against me & I crack

awakened, my eyes search for a Dionysian island
while clouds brush through
a mist behind a mist behind a mist
where a lone boat drifts

my sigh causes the air around me to tremble
& I have no voice to call for happiness

a stained sun bows to my despair
& I am a birth abandoned in a desert full of unheard murmurs

a pearly wind reminds me softly to fly away
into the mist behind the mist behind the mist
where water falls into a bouquet of evening dusk

gazing into a nail-scratched wall of madness
I hear a voice repeating,
"where is the other shore?"
"where is the other shore?"

"once, only once or once more!"

I cry back to the voice until my cry carves
an emptiness into the blue of eternity

- after all,
the sky's vastness always runs parallel
to my never-proclaimed whispers   -

"I will never rest until I find you"

a fire flowering in my trapeze-memory gathers
songs I have never sung when ornaments on my body,
ancient & new, flicker to the breath you swallow

oh Orpheus!

"once, only once & once more…"
I cross the ocean full of chattering layers of foam
to reach one shore & the other & the other still further away

when darkness breaks into an interval of TIME

I uselessly force myself to ring a bell again & again
in my throat to tell you that I am "here"

ANATOMY OF MELANCHOLY II

do not
press
your heart
onto
mine
for
my heart
is yours

do not
drop
an agonized
intimacy
into
my memory
for
my memory
is yours

ANATOMY OF MELANCHOLY III

love-melancholy loves love's power
& extends its idleness to the dead end
but never asks for charity

beauty causes symptoms of love
& cures its ill-favoured allurements

a river runs through all cities, small or large,
where lust never shows contempt
for despair nor jealousy

CROSSING LINES

for Sarah Sze

CROSSING LINES   (FOR SARAH SZE)

1. *Liquid to Solid*

on the day of gray on gray,
I walk into the moment = Space/Time.

wearing an unpolished pair of old shoes,

I cross lines
to reflect on
the humming of the (un)organized reality
of our natural history

trapped in eternity.

snapping salt crystal beans out of a pod,
I neatly place a model structured after me:
a mixture of all the shapes/contents/forms/meanings
of the moment,

on the alter
which is leaning forward (for "what"?)
to finish the motion (of "when"?).

2. *Colors*

white on gray.
white on deep blue sea.
white & red on gray.

red/blue/orange woven into air.

white on white.
(dead) white on (live) black.

yellow light
cast
by red shade.

black on red.

big empty footsteps
in solidified liquidity.

3. *Mirroring*

I see a light
mirroring itself
without me (the observer)
participating
in the process.

holding dust,
alphabets collected
according to their own obscure inborn purposes

rest in tiny boxes.

when a feather settles itself
in mid air
as realistic as stenciled remains of flowers,

a pebble/pebbles
sit(s) naturally purposeless
with sounds silenced

on a cushion of emptiness.

4. *Colors, Again*

let's not talk of green.
(poor) green, how much I want you
(poor) green.

yellow?
let's give it back
to the sun & luna(cy).

gray on gray,
mirroring the ceiling
becomes a floor.

a fractured remembrance of the past
becomes the future
which does not exist.

relating to unspoken metaphysics,

a red ladder,
red plants,
a red column,
red lines,
a red rod,
a red inexhaustible pain = joy,

a red tool,

anything red holds things
together.

5. *Something Empty*

somebody left an empty bottle.

here.

I squat down to hear the ripple of a breeze.

reflected on something solid once liquid,

air moves to remind me

that I am

here.

6. *Something Empty, Again*

I hear dust humming on the wall.

I am pleasantly alone & warm.

I keep my breath inside me,   so,

nothing

>   will
>   fall
>
>   apart.

another empty bottle appears on the other side of the
wall.

an island.

7. *Footsteps*

>   I enjoy the rhythm I make out of my footsteps
>   walking up the stairway.
>
>   *"Please, pass me the salt & pepper, please!"*
>
>   feeling no sense of guilt,
>   stepping on the constellations of our consciousness,
>
>   I walk stairways farther to *"Heaven,"*
>   where essential nutrients are stored safely
>   in capsules for the next generation.

8. *Speechless*

>   water trapped
>   in a tiny bag
>   forms
>   its shape
>   according to
>   its own nature.

where am I?
who am I?

who are you?

wind blows
as I face
dust/light
instead of
dust/darkness.

here,

an identity of (whatever)
becomes
more persuasive.

sharing the moment of "where,"

we are all

speechless.

9. *Salt of the Earth*

salt of the earth
starts
to fall
on
us

as we kick
"Lights of America"

to cause

some
lightening.

shall I carry an umbrella?
shall I open my mouth
to say something?

being horizontal/vertical,

we all learn
to measure
our intensions
to see things
by observing *"Reality"*
in a slightly more
accurate mode.

Cactus; dead or alive.
Clay; burnt or raw.
a key here is
to keep some order
even in the most
destructive moments.

let's play a game of *"Go"*!

as we collect
both dust & dirt
secretly gathered
in the forgotten corner
of a rectangular room.

a grain of salt,
stripped,
duped
& lifted,

plug/unplugs
itself
from

the earth.

6 FOR L.B.

poems for Louise Bourgeois

C'EST LE MURMURE DE L'EAU QUI CHANTE

1. sitting alone
   on a flat stern wooden chair
   perfect in size for the moment's metaphysical need
   I fade into the sun-lit emptiness
   of passing time

2. there is a ⎣⎦ mirror
   in the middle of the room
   where I greet a stranger
   walking into a view
   warped & wavy
   as if (s)he is a reversed reflection
   of our buried common memories

3. trying my best
   not to be too conscious of
   the (un)intentional malice of our species
   sung by murmuring water
   in an (un)familiar tongue

   with my courteous honesty
   I write a concise atlas of world history
   blind-folded
   avoiding to filter it through self-effacing shadows
   of our pathology

4. instead of calling for MOTHER
   at the height of the gripping excitement
   of Mobius-strip-like day dreaming
   I clearly proclaim my self-identity, shouting,
   "I am never a sentimentalist!"

the precision of four clear-cut 90-degree angled corners
of the room tells me nonchalantly
"Privacy is always in public domains or vice-versa."

5.   I am not ALICE
      my first name ends with "O" instead of "E" or "A"

leaving the room
I join 2 palms
to make a circle

PROGRESSION

1.
Don't be sticky!
Don't lean on me!
Don't be stuffy!

The fabricated bareness
of our manufactured silence
resounds
like an echo
in an open field

Please touch me instead
when no one is around
& pretend that you are
in the midst of climbing a mountain

2.
"Up" or "Down"
One must work hard
to make one's words
stand out clearly
stitched (in mud)
as one thread

3.
Sewing
colors
together

I sleep
inside
soft
skin

(Do not)
abandon
me
despite
your preference
for a generically
picturesque
value
system

We can still share
the same air
although we have
definite differences
in the way
we see things

REJECTION

Capital letters stuck
behind the back of my neck
describe nothing of
my shock, a map of my Utopia,
in vain

I've lost my tongue, eyes,
even my terry-clothed head
& a wagging tail

"It is urgent—"

In order to save my conscience
from the melt-down
I, for the first time, welcome
every aspect of human vulgarity
with no hesitation or remorse

On the contrary
with plenty of joy
I scratch the metaphysical outline
of my daily life
to give some space
for applause

for YOU

OBESE/BULIMIC/ANOREXIC

an
aging
man
in a black
coat
stares
right into
the eyes
of
the young
girl
in
his
arms

in public

he whispers
to her
maliciously
that
he knows
how
to
be
sweet

COUPLE

1.   a man & a woman
resting on each other's moist skin
grasp for a feathery comfort
wearing nothing but air

I am an orphan
with no biography
who witnesses
their slow vertical flowering

seduced by the neutrality of light
I pay an extraordinary attention
to my crumbling shadow
scattered on the cold hard floor

suddenly
I burst into laughter
as I finally figure out
the secret of my origin

2.   hanging
in the room
where darkness & light
mean nothing
but a clear-cut precision
of 90-degree angled four corners
in a rectangle space
a man & a woman
breathe the modest silence
together alone
as they recede
into their own (waltzing) shadows

CELL XXV   (THE VIEW OF THE WORLD OF THE JEALOUS WIFE)

she circles 'round & 'round
a circling shadow
of her own headache
wrapped in & protected by
a floral patterned philosophy

she breathes the absence
of head, arms, legs & voice
& enjoys her weightless burden
of her being as heavy as
the world she lives in

she blows a coarse whistle
abruptly when she is in the mood
on the back(side) of her emotions
as she imagines the shoe sizes
of other women

she never gets enough
of mellow bitterness
of gossip's aftertaste

she indulgently fails
to unlock the door of her "cause & effect"

twelve blue bells ring do-re-mi
twelve months pass by quickly crisscrossed

"A globe & balls, they share the same form, don't they?
she casts an anxious question

to her barrel-shaped vanity
every morning
she wakes up
next to her husband

GIOTTO DETAILS/FRAGMENTS

1. *To a Woman*

Woman,

why are you musing
so pensively
on something so intangible,
wrapped in a pale green robe
cheek on arm
arm resting on your drawn-up knee

as a pliant sea breeze strokes
your ancient feet?

Woman,

why do you let tears fall
so indifferently
as you fall into
an ungraspable melancholy

in the pre-dusk air?

2. *Mourning*

The glance of a woman
in black, tonight,
is darker than the shadow
cast by a lone leaf
flirting with darkness.

3. *Journey*

Two men walk together;
one in vermilion
& the other in cerulean blue.

"Friend, look at those shining rocks!"
the man in vermillion points
at a soaring mountain.

"Brother, take this fragrant breeze!"
says the man in blue spreading his arms
fully in the bright air.

"How long have we been marching
together like this?

&

where are we headed to?"

Two men share the same cordial breath.

Majestically
leaving themselves
to the flow of the air,

they kick a shadow of uncertainty
hanging stealthy before them
on the course of their journey

as if it were
a pebble.

4. *Pensée*

Tears pour down
when one thinks of
why we rest our cheeks
in our hands as we muse
over pensive thoughts.

How many are born;
how many are bidding
farewell to the sky above;
& how many are bending
their fragile & soft fingers
tenderly as they droop their heads

in the transiency of this moment?

Ah.

Why does one stare
at a condensed point in darkness
when one lets oneself fall
into a pensive thought?

5. *Prayer*

There is always a moment
when one surely
wants to reflect the self
on the serene surface
of flowing water,
at least once a day.

There is surely a sparkling moment
when everyone wants
to throw the self away
in order to merge the pains
of life with the spirit of water
to erase it.

At such a moment,

there is always
a cruel wind blowing
behind the ears
& a remote star shining
above one's head.

FOR A PAINTER

FOR A PAINTER 1

I eat
Bread &
Dutch cheese
Every day

I think of
Vincent &
Other Dutch painters
& their lives

FOR A PAINTER 2

I am a painter
Who does not paint
But I love color
Form & line

Solid = Void
Is my nick name
For a long time

FOR A PAINTER 3

I was outside
Of myself
When I was born
Since then
I've learned

How to go
In & out

I am still
Very small
But I know
My voice
&
I love
To sing

FOR A PAINTER 4

Paint brushes
Paint tubes
Paint sticks

Space

Color is
Floating
Everywhere
In a place
Where
I have
Never been
Or
Never seen

FOR A PAINTER 5

I am married
To a poet
&
His father
Was
A painter

He
Painted
The interiors
Of
Other people's
Houses
&
He was
Very
Good

FOR A PAINTER 6

One day
I will
Paint
Like
Others do
To
Paint
Like
No others can

Do

&

Then
I will call
Myself
A
Dancer

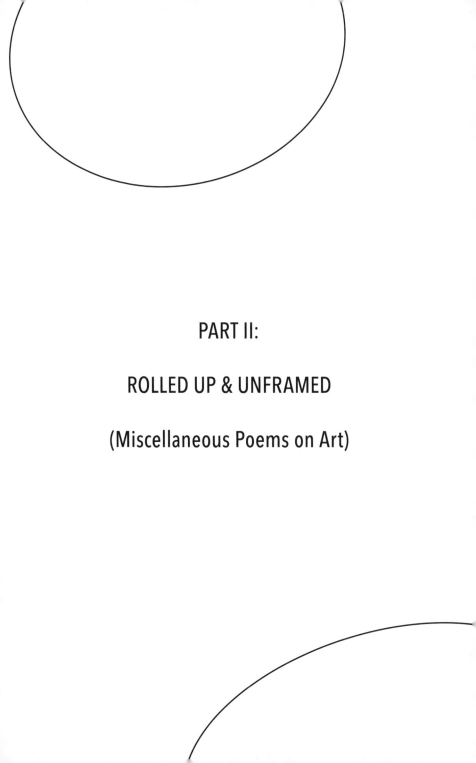

PART II:

ROLLED UP & UNFRAMED

(Miscellaneous Poems on Art)

NOVEMBER SUNDAY I

"It's a subdued Clyfford Still," you said,
reacting to me pointing at
yellow ginkgos & a red oak
overlapping each other

on the way to the market (battle ground)
we heard a man saying to a woman
"you are such a bad girl!"

on the way home from the market (battle ground)
we saw a man reading *The Great Gatsby*
in a tiny patch of sunlight

NUDE STUDY (FOR GERMAINE KRULL & OTHER WOMEN PHOTOGRAPHERS OF THE WEIMAR ERA)

1.

in a modern building,
there is a small room

where

she sits, stands & lives

it has a tiny peephole
for her
to see the world,
through
inner & outer,

but,

there is not
too much space
for her
to walk around

she studies a nude:
a naked psyche
of one's being;
an untainted body-surface
to hold the whole

light & shadow
take their chances

bravely,
caressing
its soft curves &
round footsteps

2. *a variation on the theme*placeholder

through a tiny hole
she sees things, air,
an image of a shell,
a plate, other women
& men

she merges herself into
an objective quietness of
thread & spools

caressing the fundamental tone of life,

she faces
history

2 flowers bend themselves
this way & that
as she dives
deeper & deeper
into the sea

BIRTH   (MICHELANGELO: ST. MATTHEW 1506)

a man is born
out of a rock

a man

who has slept an eternal sleep
in a heavy rock
packed tightly with a cold density
in a solid void

now

awakens

turning his tender ears
to the ancient sounds of a harp
coming from far away

a man is born
out of a rock

and stands distinctly
with the clear color of his skin
burning brightly
in the grand darkness

out of an extremely quiet rock
a man is born

and now accurately

steps a step of dew
into the reality where
the wind blows

FILIPPINO LIPPI & HIS CIRCLE

miniver & squirrel hair,
goose or chicken feathers,
burned wood/willow sticks = charcoal
to draw lines & make shadows

bread crumbs in a shell
to erase "what's not there"

powdered lead with water & gum arabic
to highlight the breath
& to be oxidized eternally

an artist saw
the head of an elderly man turned to the right
with downcast eyes of Renaissance
modern

a young man is always young
all through history
until he ages

crisscrossing made darkness
to show depth then
& so it does in our century

going home,
I face
the head of a young man turned to the left downward
on the subway
whether we notice it or not
time never fails to surpass itself

2 FOR C. D. FRIEDRICH

NEAR THE HORIZON A WIND MILL TURNS

on the vast green spreading earth
a face of a man lies down
a tired face of a man
who suffers dark sufferings
lies down

chaos filtering through
a soft sun-beaming sky
deepens the shadow
on a man's forehead

near the horizon
a wind mill turns
near the horizon
horses run
near the horizon
a man's tears turn into love

on a vast spreading crowd of rocks
the voice of a woman lies down
a wet voice, bending over
some unrealistic tenderness
lies down

melancholy falling
from the day ending sky
adds a serious pain
to her voice

her voice waves
&
a man's face gets distorted

near the horizon
darkness burns
near the horizon
stars sway
near the horizon
time dances

.   .   .

wind rings trees
&
night visits the world

.   .   .

the piercing stillness of night
cures wounds of a man
the stillness of night
cures wounds of a woman

near the horizon
roses bloom
near the horizon
a breeze rustles
near the horizon

the sea appears

A LITTLE AWAY FROM THE POINT WE SEE

a little away from the point we see
our lives are making
a thick ice-ridged wreckage
of ashes, sweat & some whimsical meditative senses

a little away from the point we see
our dreams are laughing a low laugh

a little away from the point we see
our joy is making a thick ice-ridged wreck
over the wreck

a little away from the point we see
an evening breeze passes
an evening bell tolls

upon the mass of an eternal contradiction of humanity
breathing low & secretively
stars flow
stars run

the agony of stars is far
& our blood is the sadness of summer weeds

a little away from the point we see
our skepticism with deflated objects
is making an arrogant shadow

a shadow leads to tumult
tumult builds senselessness

senselessness draws an empty line in the sky
a man & a woman go back & forth
between the sadness beyond extreme ends
of their lives & the past
& they wait together
for a desolate morning

a little away from the point we see
a vegetative truth grows thickly
with some abstract power
without saying a word

a little away from the point we see
cynicism itself is laughing nihilistically

a little away from the point we see
our shameless confusion is making
a thick ice-ridged wall

a little away from the point we see
our shadows are making one serious map

a little away from the point we see
our hearts want to make an eternal departure

a little away from the point we see
a ship hoists its sail
waiting for us

a ship dedicates its heart
to the stillness of waves

a little away from the point we see

hearts wait for a departure
hearts wait for a departure

a little away from the point we see
hearts wait for a departure quietly
an evening breeze roams heavily
the sound of a bell dreams

a little away from the point we see
night kisses us

a little away from the point we see
night kisses us

MODEL   (FOR ADA KATZ)

another day
when clouds move
with a perfect pitch
for their shape & volume

in perfect light

she walks on a straight line
implicitly identical
to herself in his painting

ANOTHER STORY

Frida Kahlo painted a still life with watermelons as her last painting with an inscription that said, "Viva la Vida." Following her, Diego Rivera too painted a still life with watermelons as his last painting. That was his way of showing his love, respect & regrets to her in the ultimate expression. Frieda's watermelons were as round as balls and Diego's watermelons were oval.

TRACING TIME WITH 2BS & 3BS   (FOR MORGAN O'HARA)

Being is Time. —*Dogen*

1.

I don't remember exactly when, but I remember the circumstances under which I met Morgan. It was in Soho, when Soho was still Soho. Warhol walked around with a camera in his hands taking snapshots of the weekend crowds on W. Broadway; SAMO *(known already by his real name)* was still around; so were Cage & Nam June *(they were the best; so humble & so sweet)*. Ted (Joans) & Jack (Micheline) used to fly in & out magically like seasoned migrating birds *(oh, I wish I had their "Wander Lust" & their courage!)*. We *(steve & I)* used to walk to see Johns & Rauschenberg in the neighborhood galleries after buying milk & bread @ M&O *(amazing! they are still there!)*. Chelsea & Brooklyn were just the names of general districts of the city. Nobody (except the "pioneering" artists who moved to those areas for cheaper spaces) went there for "art" yet. It was the mid-80s.

It was at some evening music event @ 420 W. Broadway which housed big galleries such as Castelli & Sonnabend. I'm sure the event took place on the first floor. Was it Threadgill or Jon Gibson? I don't remember that too well either.

In the space, I saw a woman sternly focused on what was going on in front of us, moving both hands rather maniacally & intensely but in a totally concentrated manner. In both of her hands, there were bundles of 2Bs & 3Bs gathered by chance operation. Her eyes never moved away from the subject except for the moments when she tried to grab a different bundle of graphite pencils. Her eyes were her hands constantly & it went on like this 'till the music ended.

I walked up to her & saw the resulting "work." I was curious but too shy to talk to her. I am quite sure it was Jackson Mac Low *(oh, I miss him so much!)* who introduced us. Since then we kept running into each other whenever/wherever some good music event took place. Soon we became friends. She told me of the childhood she spent with her family in post WWII Japan, around the time I was born & grew up. She showed me her photographer mother's work which chronicled Japan & its people's lives & faces in this post-devastation period. The Japan connection bonded us more.

We both live in the same area not too far & still occasionally run into each other as we used to do.

2.
What a "wild" idea it is to give up both paws eternally to free them from the slavery of holding the body against the earth! Pithecanthropus Erectus *(when was the last time I listened to Mingus?)*! What a "wild" thing to have those front paws in the service of whatever we want to do with them!

Morgan traces Time in real Time; holding 2Bs & 3Bs in her freed paws; sharing the moment/space with other human beings who do things with their ex-paws. Hands of a farmer's wife digging asparagus in Germany *(I love asparagus! it's almost the season)*; hands of a friend knitting a sweater in her Greenwich Village tenement apt. *(what color & pattern did the yarns make?)*; hands of a poet reciting his poems & a pianist's hands accompanying him in a downtown NYC cafe *(ah, they work so well together. I always love their duet)*; hands of a street paver setting B & W paving stones in Macao *(the street must look pretty much like a game of "Go")*; hands of a sound engineer & a percussionist performing in Chile *(electricity & organic instruments in unison)*; hands shaking & wrapping noodle balls in China *(magic!)*; hands of an avant-garde musician playing his instrument in an uptown NYC concert hall *(steve & I were there)*; hands of workers at the Furukawa fish market in Aomori, Japan *(those hard-working people of the north)*…

She travels & meets people & draws, tracing Being = Time in real Time = Being.

3.
in a (white) square of void,
a quivering, quickening, indifferent notion of our being = time
forms a graphite cloud: gray on gray.

who are we? are we here? when is now?

a tiny dot/a thin line
appears, moves & disappears
as if nothing matters
to anything or to anyone

except

"thusness."

A RITUAL   (FOR CHANTAL REGNAULT)

in mud
our bellies
become waves & wavelets

our eyes shine
wetter than ever

our desire & despair
quiet

in mud
we do not
sing in words

REMEMBERING: A MEMORIAL READING FOR RAY JOHNSON AT
BUECKER & HARPSICHORDS, 465 W. BROADWAY

a brick wall
was painted white
from the floor
to the ceiling
& there were
a couple of potted plants—
the color green was
impressively dark
& made them
look almost
fake & dead

2 poets read

a few late comers
stood silently & shyly
by the door

behind the elevator door
a rumbling noise
similar to an old coal-mining truck
went up & down
faintly
on & off

I thought of south & north

1st poet
had a valley
between his brows

2nd poet
had a simply-complicated
river running
in his voice

a lone glass water pitcher
on the podium
made a summer-lake-like
reflection
on the wall

1st poet said

*"stars are uncanny
but bright"*

an exquisite evening sky
I marveled at
on the way there
came vividly back
inside my eye lids

.   .   .

I was extraordinarily
conscious of eyes in general—
sitting on a green chair
listening to them read
I particularly thought of
my own eyes I saw this morning
in the mirror
which drifted away

into an unexpected direction
when I tried to look into them
to see what was there behind the door

1ˢᵗ poet's hand
moved almost unconsciously
on his face a few times
as if he was brushing off a shadow
cast on his profile

I kept wandering into
R.J.'s hinged pieces of wood
& could not stop being
fascinated by their small voices

.   .   .

"firm like   a tree—
a fruit of trueness—
something solid & non-abstract
to share—"

2ⁿᵈ poet explained

his writing hand looked photographic, copying
its own image on the glass box
standing next to him
which contained a glass jar—
a memory of a scene of lined up laboratory jars
filled with liquid & innards, dark & crippled,
kept coming to mind
& I felt sick & choked up
but maintained joyfulness

.   .   .

I tried to visualize
someone's physical features
such as the shapes of his hands/fingers
& the way he stood
leaning with a slightly self-conscious melancholy, etc

what else?

.   .   .

"*the ground was white
marble dust mixed with
sand from the beach—*"

a voice in some film
I saw a few days ago
kept circling in me

I wondered how & what
R.J. saw & tasted
when he was wrapped
in the eternal sea
he dived into

people disappear
as if they were never
here

.   .   .

social chatting kept us
long in the space—

when we walked out
to the street
we were as light as
a small packet
forwarded to no-one
particular

we said good-bye
to each other dispersing
into whichever direction

we preferred
to take

I AM VERMILION   (FOR ANGELA VALERIA)

I am new born.

My face is painted by an artist from the remote past,
who lived on a remote island,
where the coming & receding tides acted as a role of God.

I have not yet learned to speak,
but, I know Tranquility well.
The splendor of my sacred conversation
with a soft defused courtesy & generosity of unfinished fate
is so blinding & full that I know I am nothing.

With a hazy warmth prevailing inside me,
holding a gentle flower as new as I, just born out of mud,
I learn to be a perceiver of Sound.

Beyond the senses,
beyond imagination,
beyond repeatedly counted uncountable dawns & dusks,
I begin to hear the lamentation of the unaltered framework
of the mosaic world.

I am Vermilion.

I hold a luminous pearl fallen from the landscape of the sky.
I hold a wrathful horse-head.
I hold a sword, an umbrella, a water jar & an axe.
I am fierce-eyed & pure.
I am infinitely cloaked with leaves of the 4 seasons
as the infinite of the infinites
remains infinitely alone.

Tearing the repeated history of the island,
scattered all over the walls surrounding Void,
I spit Vermilion syllables emptying my hands further.

I am a wheel, starting to turn, without form,
to reflect the sun in a pool of water.

I am Vermilion.

I am just born.

A VOICE THAT CRAWLS IN THE SKY   (FOR V. V. G.)

Every thinkable botany
has never looked so bestial.

I hear a voice crawling
in the sky, witnessing an almond tree
blossoming. Every single flower becomes
one with the trembling voice.

Before we talk of our hearts, minds,
even our hands & feet, let's pay
attention to the pureness of the artist.

Let's be moved by our own gentle senses
of respecting a shadow cast in a bowl
of meekness.

Left/right/back/front.

Birds, 3 of them,
proudly & simply
sit on a branch.

EVERYBODY   (42ND ST. ART PROJECT 1993)

on a solid surface of an indifferently hardened material

2 men sit
think
rest

on the same mid-afternoon-sun-lit surface

a woman joins
their vacuumed solitude
she seems to want nothing

chairs float
empty, wired to the air
painted silver, purple, red & gold
with nobody on them

the sky is blocked
by a giant yellow billboard
that says EVERYBODY

weaving a series of one liners
into our life's breaths
one after another

we skeptically try to
cheer ourselves up

shoes glued to a temporary eternity
walk into an empty theater;

they look warm with
human sweat

we mirror ourselves
on an affordable looking glass

every day

but

we still don't know
who we are

MISSION   (WRITTEN FOR JCW WHILE LISTENING TO RS TALK ON
THE REVIEW PANEL DISCUSSION WITH JG & BS MODERATED BY DC @
NA, FEB. 8, 2008)

1.
"What does it mean?"

Don't mention the books on aesthetics
locked inside the antiquarian book cases
if you know the answer.

In the room heated by a bleached brightness,
familiar images of interior scenes of our psyche
spoil themselves & become twisted flesh dusted with sand.

They warp forcefully,
begging for attention to highlight human oddities.

I listen & write without thinking,
without making any sense,
being part of the crowd.

To my left,
there is an insect-like buzzing of ART.

To my right,
there is the rectangular blankness of art.

I listen to forget
everything I hear.

2.

Evolution of an idea on "observation"
transmutes everything to nothing
& nothing back to everything again.

Divided between 2 camps,
I easily fall into a sympathetic mood
for anyone who knows
how to say "Please!" properly
in a squeaking voice
at the right moments & under the right circumstances.

It's no surprise that some kind of stylized
behavioural restlessness of an artist
can be read as a sign of apathy
as blunt as books with no titles.

A biomorphic reflection
of formalism, classicism,
post-modern humanism
& unsolved social issues etc,
all mix up with the forced absurdity
of pseudo UBU philistines.

We are not doing anything but rewriting the Book of Job.

All the rest is just sad sexuality.

3.
He is not looking back (to the glorious past).

He just wants access to multiple forms
of correct availabilities un–delayed
by measured assimilations of concepts
of art in general.

There is a slightly broken blind
in the room, unnoticed & unrelated
to anyone who claims to be an artist.

"Effects only! Please!"
a projected argument over the amplified voice of a
masterpiece
jolts its tone only to participate
in the race for an allegorical theatricality.

4.
"INFINITY SHOE SHINE!"
shouts the fatigued humanism
of plenary civilization
idealized by a great work of art = ART.

Landscape of ISM(s)
& (un)gilded history
of (in)sanity & horror
mimic "anamorphoses"
of "how"
similar to "retardataire"
of "what & why"
with a radical ambition.

Occasionally & impartially,
a fair Q & A gives away
clues to the secret of the potential distinction
between "to observe" & "to be observed"

"Let's take a frame home
& leave the content behind!"

5.
Relatively traumatic changes
in the miscalculation of "what it means"
cause the birth of a beautiful new hat.

Under the snow-less sky,
snow-covered roofs still
an abbreviated sense of MISSION
in order to feed the entire over-exposed world.

"It's a good deal!
I'd better look for a seat!"

Someone blasts my ears
to nil.

JCW: Jeffrey Cyphers Wright
RS: Robert Storr
JG: James Gardner
BS: Barry Schwabsky
DC: David Cohen
NA: National Academy

VOTRE SERVICE "CALTEX" #1   (FOR BERND & HILLA BECHER)

a function develops into a new purpose
& a new purpose, forming triangles & circles warped & bent,
delivers goods & fuels smoothly
to our tables to fill our longings
for "Happiness & Comfort"

a function digs & presses dirt,
stands next to winter-spring weeds,
remembered or forgotten,
wrapped altogether
in oxidized breaths
of a gray day

"Beauty has nothing to do with us."

bricks, piled up, want
walls, roofs & windows with cracked transparency
to be completed

a function leads us to a new function
to develop to make disconnected tubes & sunken tanks
to mirror images of our endless boredom & greed
to fill gaps between two sentences
we rarely speak

a grand service for you & me
designed to polish & dye
our decency to be human & overpoweringly civil
comes full circle a few times
before it comes back to face us

at the starting point
as blank & mute factory beams

VOTRE SERVICE   "CALTEX" #2

it is like my face
or your face
or my feet
or your feet

sullen, chubby & comfortable

it is like my needs
or your needs
or my pride
or your pride

gray, mute & obedient

VOTRE SERVICE   "CALTEX" #3

a horizon views
the earth
& its structural completeness—

our identity stands, forgotten,

no moon
no sun

in the background

CENTRE BEAUBOURG

art does not need
(to have)
a proper noun,

a poet said

DELICIOUS SOLITUDE (AFTER FRANK BRAMLEY'S PAINTING WITH THE SAME TITLE)

Hush!

Try to calm your desires down
Learn to ask no questions

Her name
Her age
Her family

Do they really matter?

She is reading
under light/shadows of early summer trees
in the midst of an abundance
of the season's idle afternoon fragrance

They call a woman a flower
but in this delicious solitude
flowers are a woman,
a breeze, green = blue

How hard it is for us
to stop our needs
to conquer things!

Our want to touch her dress;
to see her face under her hat;
to know something about the book
she is holding with her delicate hands
is making our 'essence' tremble

By all means
do not wake her up
from the luxurious reverie
of the moment

Learn to ask nothing

How seductive it is
to bury oneself
in this bell-shaped monotonous
clairvoyant air—!
Hush!
Do not move!
Leave her be
Leave her be

Let us leave quietly
in our modest illusion
while we can
before we break the marvel
of the moment

Leave her be
Leave her be

Let her entice
light/shadows of afternoon

fully

in her delicious solitude

ROOFTOP URBAN PARK PROJECT   (FOR DAN GRAHAM)

1.
the sure uncertainty
of not knowing
how to open
the door
puzzled me
in such a way

that I instantly
felt like I was
floating,
(or rather),
swimming
in a remote sea.

clouds looked
increasingly
non-animated
as I finally
slipped into
the dense transparency
of the air
with no effort.

when I had
an immense urge
of wanting to be
buried in nostalgia
of some kind,
an urban landscape

nonchalantly
confronted me.

"when am I?"
I muttered
to my own reflections.

2.
I see myself
seeing myself
seeing myself.

I point at myself
pointing at myself
pointing at myself.

I try to grab myself
seeing myself
pointing at myself
seeing myself.

I try to talk
to myself
with no words.

now,
I realize
that I am
standing
in the air.

3.
some endless,
opaque-transitional breath
swallowed me
with no warning.

all I could do
was to listen to
a distant lingering echo
of some kind
in the landscape.

I hesitantly sympathized
with myself
for being so heavenly helpless.

the magical aloneness
of my being
seemed almost comical
to the tormented sensitivity
of my skin
when it broke into
infinite shadow/images.

"Ah!

I want to
call out to someone!"

I so awaken,
looked up
to the sky

above me,
knowing quite surely
it was the only possible escape
from this pleasurable
contemplation

on gravity.

ROOFTOP URBAN PARK PROJECT II

I walk,

but,

this bouncing impact
to my spine
is too sensual
for me
to take.

I need to rest.

watching
people
in the distance

with an ambivalent yearning
to reach them

is like
living in a house
with no roof
where I know
I'll sleep better
than usual.

I enjoy
a sense of
vertigo.

I love to
walk on
the wall.

don't say anything!
saying "things"
might ruin
the fun.

CAVE   (FOR RANDEE SILV)

1. *Flat File*

in a cavernous darkness
of absolute fear & awe

our sense of contentment
to be "nobody"
in the world

rests

soundly

without having any sort of
dream, hope, expectation
or wish

there

no measurement
of any kind
is required

to judge

where one stands

2. Non-Symbolic Language to (Re)discover (My)self

A new breath taps
Into a cave of the vast ocean
Of forgotten gestures
In order to dictate a drama
On Art's origin
Without dense plots nor anagrams

Yellow yellowing
Black blacking
Void voiding
Line lining
Dot dotting
Form forming

Air is light

Without shadow shadowing

Stretching fully
To declare

The sacredness of Color

SPECTROHELIOGRAPHS   (FOR MIKE & DOUG STARN)

1.
the sun light/shadows the earth
& we form an identity

as flowers breathe
colors of water & air

occasionally we confuse
the intangible sense of reality
with the size of the earth

our planet

yet no matter what
rain falls to stop
the sun eclipses to reappear

& we surely live on the surface
of our mother's skin,
knowing or not knowing

2.
in the original paradise
when we were granted grace
to enter the high wheel
of (r)evolution of divine comedy
we almost felt the size of the earth

our planet

a woman glanced at a sun–ring
with her soft stern eyes
& opened her one thousand arms of Compassion

& exclaimed "How bright we are within us!"

3.
the sun flowers in darkness
when we sleep in the age
of Electrified Gods

the sun blares to the limit
of limitlessness
to eclipse to reappear
to eclipse again

we study laws & the aphorisms of physicians
to learn to content ourselves
with understanding the realistic senses
of the size of the earth

our planet

as the earth floats on a sea of clouds
nonchalantly

4.
at history's end/beginning
a shadowed figure walks
on a summer/winter day

alone

&

she whispers to herself

"Who am I?
Where do I come from?
Where am I going?"

wherever she goes
the sun flowers

whenever she whispers
the sun shadows to shine

her way

SPECTROHELIOGRAPHS II

apocalyptic
      fragments
            of paradise
                  connect us
                        to disconnect
                              ourselves
                                    from us

3 FOR LUCIAN FREUD

DOUBLE-PORTRAIT

naked
in a sweater
I sit & wonder
"why are we all here?"
but my mouth is sealed
with the weight of the question
so I just try my best to pose
as comfortable as possible
for the artist

I look at him
as if he were
a potted plant

I am very tired
but not unhappy
in this interior

soon I realize
how contemporary I am
in many senses
& I start to feel
my flesh
faintly blush

NIGHT PORTRAIT, FACE DOWN I

I want
everything
to disappear

in some lingering image
trees I saw in the afternoon
shake themselves
minutely

the voice of the artist
saying "Stay as you are!,"
a solo sound,
crawls on the floor

I don't want anything
I just want to forget myself
as I leave my body
to the seduction of silence
in the room's corner

in a vertically falling darkness
I lay down in bed, face down
clinging to my own shadow

in a lingering image, again
trees get agitated

thinking of the accurate darkness of their sap
my skin sinks heavily

as if starting on an endless long journey,
a new uncertainty
makes me feel
happy

the other side of the door
is the bottom of the sea

for an instance
original sin makes a shriek
resembling
pure love

NIGHT PORTRAIT, FACE DOWN II

I think myself fortunate
for not having imagination

leaving everything I am
to the candid materiality of the bed
I bite my skin & its history
enveloping me

in a vertically falling darkness
my pressed surface quietly
breathes

swallowing
a voice of the artist saying "Stay as you are!,"
a solo sound to share the room's silence,
I throw myself, a female who has no words

my palms,
grasping air & letting it go,
are strangely warm

flowing hair is heavy

almost losing myself totally,
I sniff its smell

innocently

SILENCE IS NOT ENOUGH   (FOR SUZAN FRECON)

earth red
terra verde
ultra marine
indigo

blue

matte or gloss

silence is not enough

I stand
in a room

full of

muted
light

★

je pense
je suis

on me pense
JE est un autre

★

to free
oneself
from uttering
words

one

has to

see/gaze
into something
without
having a reference

point

of departure/terminal

★

"here/now"
lets me
disappear

to

be

the roundness
of
colors
in

thoughts
itself

&, only there,

I hear
my voice
in my own

silence

ILLITERATE   (JAMES CASTLE: HOUSE DRAWING)

Heavy deep layers of tree after tree
& their solidified mass.
That is my voice of melancholy.

Nothing moves.

I am a chair
filled with negative spaces.

Complications of sooty floors & beams
invite me & I joyfully open the door.

House after house.
That is my face.
A face of which I have not yet known.
A language which has no words.

The earth-smelling sky.
That is the shadow of my comfort.
A secret.
A kind of remote agony.

MEMORY OF   (FOR KAZUKO MIYAMOTO)

1.
In search of lost time,

I spread a sheet of invisible mist
on the hard floor, alone at night,
to place objects of various memories;
big & small; tangible & intangible; fragile & solidified.

Soon, the floor becomes a dark ocean.

In its immensity,
I see myself as a tiny fish.

In search of lost time,

I swim,

through familiar & unfamiliar dust,
through brown bags twisted in a ritualistic form,
through stretched hard constructions of soft strings
supported by an abundance of nails,
through nonchalantly assembled weathered twigs,
through tortured sheetrock,
through mischievously erotic loose fabrics,
through obediently reformed old newspaper articles,

through *lost time,*

I keep swimming
till I lose sight of myself
in the ocean's immortal weight & immeasurable depth.

2.

Is it morning? Or afternoon? I don't know.
But I know that I am in a room
full of windows of light/shadow.

I do not hear too much sound
except for my own beating heart.

Bewildered by the fresh sensation,
I walk around the room.

Soon the room turns into a landscape, breathing,
spotted with a thick forest, a winding river, a deep valley & a
quiet meadow.

Responding to this expansive scenery,
with an innocent & natural awe,
I suddenly become a bird.

I fly, circling around the sky above
& rest my wings occasionally
on the tree branches, on the grass, on the rocks & boulders
of my life: the history of my art.

Whenever I brush against a breeze called MEMORY OF,
I un-bashfully call my first name & greet my very self,
simply saying " Hello Kazuko, how are you?"

I hear my voice echo
in unison with my lost time
in the vastness of light/shadow

ever so clearly.

MEDARDO ROSSO

a hollowed plaster cast
is a cave, where
soul breathes
the eternal

our skin is wax, & it melts
when darkness & sorrow
get too hot
to bear

A LETTER TO CHRISTINE (FOR CHRISTINE HUGHES)

Dear Christine,

This afternoon I took a walk alone, escaping from the persistent lingering heat in our small tenement apt. & a sense of the corrupted routines of everyday life that I was beginning to suffer. I hid myself under a brimmed hat & sunglasses, not just for heat protection but to make myself invisible in the world.

As I let my feet take their course with no particular destination or aim, I started to write a letter to you in mind. With no pen or paper, I let myself roam around within the flow of thoughts, talking to you. & it added some silent music to my solitary walk in the city.

Imagining you being somewhere in the country is one of my favorite things to do in every season, since doing so always delivers me a fresh pastoral air as I get stuck in the devouring life of the city. Every season brings me a different imaginary landscape you are in, but for some reason I enjoy imagining you in the summer environment the most. Maybe because of the beauty of the wildflower-blooming country-scape I envision, or maybe because of my own heightened desire to be there surrounded with a less human oriented reality.

How are you? Where are you? In the garden? In the kitchen? In the studio? In the woods? Or, in the stream? Wherever you are & whatever you are doing, I hope you are well. How is your work coming out? What are you working on now? I am doing ok, trying not to be swallowed by the city summer as much as I can. I am working on a new series which I am enjoying fully although working in an extremely small space makes the heat not so easy to take at all.

Interestingly I've never asked you this question before, but do you listen to music when you work? I do. Not all the time; but most of the time. The other night, I listened to Schumann. He is one of my favorites; especially his piano work. I love his melancholy & quiet dark fragility. I played his "Waldszenen: Forest Scenes" while I worked at night. Do you know this music?

"Entry" invites you to walk into the woods ever so gently. Your feet touch the moist cool bounciness of the earth & you are surrounded with the silent air of the forest. You pass by "Hunter on the Lookout." As you roam around, you encounter "Lovely Flowers." You soon get a bit frightened with the unfathomable mystery of the woods in "Places of Evil Fame." You keep walking & are welcomed by a "Friendly Landscape." The sky suddenly changes, threatening to shower & you run to "Shelter" to escape from getting wet. As it clears, you hear "Bird as Prophet"... & soon, you'll bid "Farewell" to the forest to return to your ordinary reality.

I love this music so much that I played it again & again as I worked, wishing it'd never end, transporting myself deeper & deeper into the forest scenes.

Christine, how long have we known each other? A long time, I know. Isn't it amazing our friendship gets more & more real despite the fact that we rarely see each other? Come to think of it, we only see each a few times a year, only briefly most of those times. I think it is incredible that seeing or not seeing has so little to do with our friendship, don't you agree? We are connected in such a special dimensional level that we do not have to perform a ritual to assure our friendship. How fascinating it is to share this kind of "pure & sincere" emotions with a friend!

As I was walking, I was amazed to realize how my eyes determined the course of my "random & free" walk. I let my feet take the lead, but actually it was my eyes that led me around. My eyes looked for the most intricate patterns of light/ shadow & the most delicious combination of blue/green: the sky & trees. I headed for & turned toward those visual elements to determine the course of my walk. "How visual I am!" I was almost shocked to re-realize that fact. The city sound/noise almost disappeared to nothing as I followed the light/shadows, colors & hues of the day. I vividly remember once you told me of your strong, almost unbearable desire to want to draw/paint people sitting across from you on a subway car on the spot! We are both born visual beings as some are born to have other preferred perceptive tendencies.

Do you know how much I love & respect your devotion to botanical art? Whenever I think of the two of us as artists, I think of icon painters of the past. You, more like a pre-Renaissance icon painter in Italy, drawing/painting flowers, weeds, trees branches, bark & seeds instead of Jesus, Virgin & angels, & I, a bit like a Tantric artist in India, doing abstraction. Through your work, you show us the miraculous truth of the Cosmos. Indeed, plants tell us of the most humble vivid beauty of this magical Universe we live in. They live & die in silence, giving them totally to the course of Nature. I love the quietness of their existence & you draw/paint their mysteries as humbly as they are.

I started to look for wildflowers in my mind as I roamed around the cityscape. *Loosestrifes; Milkweeds; Purple Cornflowers; Asters; Blazing Stars; Vervains; Bell Flowers; Gentians; Dayflowers; Butterfly-weeds; Black-eyed Susan; Queen Ann's Lace; Daylilies; Chicory; Golden Rods...* Wildflowers grow almost everywhere. In deserts, swamps, fields & mountains. Even on roadsides & in a city lot. Yes, how true. If you pay attention, you can find pastoral nature & its beauty in the city too. & how strange to realize that these flowers don't know what they are called by us & we keep calling their names without their consent!

Nothing is so mesmerizing as the colors & forms of plants. My amazement never ceases when I see their magic. Who made them? How did it happen? Where do they come from? If I ever use words such as "Spirituality" or 'Religious Emotions", I don't feel bashful using them relating to the feeling of awe I experience when I face plants & their delicate, intricate beauty. You draw/paint them, not only in the height of their lives, but also when they are dead. I love the way you depict the everlasting proof of the miracles & mysteries of the Cosmos in their remains. I too once wrote a small poem about the yellow petals of a dead sunflower. Yes, even when they are dry, those plants carry the magical sparks they are born with.

During the walk, I noticed that the city was a bit quieter than usual. Like in rain & in snow, human activities were forced to slow down to cope with Nature's reality in this overbearing persistent heat, & I enjoyed the phenomenon. & amazingly even in the extreme heat, you can detect the slight signs of the changing season. The earth is turning as I write you. Soon, before we know it, foliage will replace the blooming wildflowers in the country & in the city.

Christine, wherever you are, whatever you are doing, I hope you are enjoying the precious nectar of the season to the maximum.

& I am sure that you are doing so.

Much love always,

Yuko

CABIN IN THE COTTON III   (FOR HORACE PIPPIN)

cotton kept illuminating
a sea of daylight
even after the sun went down
to the other side
of the mountain

my wife & I
shared an identical awe
marveling at
a night cloud
but no word
was uttered
between us

SPRING

we wear floral patterns &
pretend that we are birds

who says a chair does not
talk to the sky?

mysteries of Gorky still
reject my words

HARE   (DURER 1502)

Even in the beginning of the 16th century,
there was a young man who burnt
a flame of rebellion
& there also was a hare
that crouched down thoughtfully
with his toes put together neatly.

Nothing
differs
from our century.

To the consciousness of a hare
with quivering nostrils,
either the stillness before the storm
or the light after the storm,
they are just simple paternal warmth,
& nothing else.

There is no need for anyone of us
to make his big swaying ears
a special topic.

CATEGORIZATION

since I did not go through
so-called "academic" institutions
to study art

I know
they will call me
"an outsider-artist; a self-taught visionary;
intuitive; naïve; art-brut & mad"
when I get to the market place

LUXURY   (FOR SOL LEWITT)

a hard working layman
almost always
goes to the details
of a monument
when he is enchanted by it
wholeheartedly.

a symbol
such as a circle, a triangle,
even a simple rectangle
wins him over
as he walks through it.

for a moment,
for a very short moment,
he feels as if
he owns the castle
himself.

MYSELF: SELF-PORTRAIT   (FOR EMMA BEE BERNSTEIN)

Like anybody else, out of some basic social need, I too, look at myself in a mirror quite often. Not that I love to do so, but it's just part of our "human" thing, isn't it? I don't particularly like to face my reflected self in a cornered room with harsh artificial light, in a closed wall-papered room or in a reclining position on a seemingly comfortable sofa, but, for some reason, the situation always takes place in this kind of imagined space. Ah, how much I wish I were a Narcissist, but I am not. I usually avert my glance as quickly as possible before "she" grasps it since I know that she knows me better than I know her. She is bigger, more powerful & unfathomable. I am much more fragile & so little compared to her.

> *Faith/Fate*
> *Same/Sane*
> *History/Her Story/My Story*
> *Singles/Sidings of a One Story House in Brooklyn*

> *Camellias   Blooming   in a Concrete Garden*

Although I like to avert my glance, I love to caress the breath of devouring whispers of whatever room I am in. Disappearing into the floral pattern of the wallpaper or in a costume made of cast out suburban plaids, I erase the boundary of my being to be myself. I once told my dear friend that I was not curious about what's behind the wall, but about the wall itself & what I was looking for was not who/what I was, but what I was made of. But I don't think she got what I meant. Fortunately I have an abundant, anonymous desire to keep myself from playing doll's house in a conventional sense. I want to keep a healthy distance from "Feminism & Fashion" as much as possible.

a Tree/Trees
  an Apple/Apples
    Fake/Fate

      a Tree on a Rock

Recently I have developed an interesting new practice for being a bit tougher, so I can face "her" better when I look at myself in a mirror. I'm reading Sade to learn to be a Juliette rather than a Justine. I am born sweet like Justine & love sexy things like Juliette. I finally realized that I need to overcome my sweetness to create a better balance in this life. This afternoon, I saw a landscape of the city I grew up blazing in pre-dusk glory, but I couldn't hear its voice since I was in front of a muted wall of liquefied air that divided it from me. Amazingly, I felt unaffected by my inability to break through the wall & still enjoyed seeing what my eyes saw & it so felt good.

a Black Dress/My Girl Friends
  Lights in My Mouth/a Skelton in the Mirror

    a Girl/a Human
      a Woman/a Human

        an Island in the Water

AFTERNOON FLOWER: A SONG (FOR HOWARD HODGKIN)

I have no name.
The name they gave me
is not
mine.

I do not move,
nor talk,
although I have so many lovely things
I'd love to share with others.

I grow to stand
& will die in seeds
to grow
again.

He is looking at me
& I know that
he knows that
I am looking at him, too!

Oh, what a day!
It is afternoon!

We are both bleeding
out of joy!

Will I miss him
when he passes through me?

Sure! I will!
I will cry definitely, clearly & brightly, then.

LAST SUPPER   (LEONARDO DA VINCI)

with an air-conditioned cross behind
& a rock hanging by the side
a table stretches enough
to be an ambiguous horizon—

13, in the end, becomes 15

there

no one eats anything
but words
with occasional sipping
of silent water

KANDINSKY IN HIS STUDIO   (NO. 36 AINMILLERSTRASSE, MUNICH)

I wonder
if you had a phone
there, in your studio, where
I see a calendar
which says 11.24.
& a tiny pocket watch
sitting close
to your right shoulder

a goddess & angels, abundant
with wings, modest & still
pencils & pens
in a small clay jar, slow
grazing horses
in a rainbow field
forever protect you
& your mission
when you soak yourself
in the afternoon light

of meditation

alone

icons of $\infty = life = death = life = death = life = \infty$
will soon emanate
their pagan passion
brightly when the day
rests itself in its

infinite nothingness

with you

being a part of it

2 FOR DEGAS

UNFINISHED LANDSCAPE   (AFTER DEGAS)

a twisted willow
in the mist

beached boats
in the twilight

an icy wind
on a cliff

we walk & walk & walk
to the end of an unfinished landscape
to look for the shadows of our footsteps

before the storm
after the storm

on an island in the sea
on rocks in the mountain

we whisper to cry to talk
to ourselves

in silence

and with good-will
to caress
our own unfinished histories

DANCERS IN BLUE   (DEGAS 1898)

Under the ambiguity
of the stage wing light,
dancers start to sink
into their own reflections.

Each sigh, responding
to each luminosity & shade,
draws them idling
in the lake in woods
hidden away from the city.

The accuracy of tensing & loosening of ankles.
A healthy agility of shoulder blades.
A brilliantly defiant sense of erected back bones.
& tender muscles.
& skin.

How can one define a simile
that says "body physics supports a soul's stroll"
out loud?

In each of their sober sentiments,
dancers preparing the smooth lightness & their strength,
as if in a dream,
have no consciousness
of their body physics.

The sense of reality of their costumes
shares the color of a trembling blueness
of the late summer sky

as it melts into the clarity of
their young & tied up hair.

At such moments
before the opening of the stage,
in the midst of the rustles
from the other side of the curtain
& the orchestra's tuning,

the bitterness of Life
loses the seat
to boost its pride
forever.

X   (RICHARD SERRA: OUT-OF-ROUND)

I hear him saying
"Head Up! Straight Up!"
running back & forth in the hallway.

I bend my neck back at 90 degrees
to hold my bleeding nose up.

I am standing
in the center of a white square room
surrounded by
10 'out of round' black circles.

I am secretly ecstatic.

sky pours down
filtering itself
through triple shades.

I am alone.

slowly circling
along with black circles
thickened with black on black nothingness,
I keep repeating to myself
in a slightly unconscious mind,
"Don't think of the sun! Don't think of the sun!"

As I retreat
into a familiar childhood nostalgia,

numbers start
at 0
& stop
at 9.

EXTREME SANITY   (FOR BARBARA KRUGER)

1.
as if we were
dealing cards
we put bits & pieces
of our extreme sanity
in front of us
to make sense
out of it

opening a cloudy door
we walk into Mary's cave
on the weekend

push me
a little harder
so I feel
like you & you
feel like them
& they feel like
me

push me
a little more
I like to be
likable to like
anyone who likes
to feel, think & see
like I do

"God!"

I'm so bored
"Jesus!"
I'm so unimpressed

our never-ending arguments
over moral values & aesthetics
have gone stale, passé
& overrated
to the dead end

2.
fear not for we fear
only for our darkened fear
to protect
our own well-being

"better him/her than me"
middle-class
& petite-bourgeoisie
walk hand in hand
everywhere we go
we snapshot posterity
for our fragile & sensitive memories
to keep

3.
as if EVIL was
something like
unwanted hair
on our bodies
we keep
searching & searching

to reach to its root
in order to terminate it

but we only end up
seeing our god-shaped images
on the green green grass
of the next door neighbor's luxury

to be nothing, broken & empty
to be everything, perfect & stuffed

here in a world
of extreme sanity
burping & spitting
is more popular
& well-practiced
than breathing

who is HE, anyway?

4.
push me
a little harder
push me
a little more
don't whip me
don't honk after me
I am good,
pure & innocent
& am as happy as a lark
I pray for HEAVEN
if I am not too sleepy

& I ignore HELL
most of the time

sky & dirt
cross-bred,
scorched & hated
try to shoot
a big gun shot
to eternity
to make an immortal mark
of out dated machismo
for the sake of
our name,
our blood,
our metaphors
& our kin

"Why doesn't GOD destroy SATAN?"

5.
in the world
burdened by
a millennium of glory
we hail for
EQUALITY & FREEDOM
on the basis
of self-assertive benefits

soda pop & baseball caps
as our shared emblems
we cheer for
our holy hierarchy

look as I do
think as I do
smile as I do
believe as I do
push, spit & burp
as I do

as masses, a mob, the general public
& unique individuals
we work as hard
as ants do
to get a bite
of crushed bits & pieces
of out-of-season tropical fruits

after all
we are made in HIS image

6.
heavy snow
has been falling
on our tenement roof/floor—

to discuss
QUALITY OF LIFE
has been a taboo
in our small shoe box house
for a long time

gray, black, white & red

more & more & more

we enjoy pretending
our supposed-to-be INNOCENCE
in this poly-cell-eternity

an increasing fog
has been covering
our thinly constructed paper walls

more & more & more
we forget half-heartedly
that we've never learned
how to turn the switch
on & off

7.
Who is HE, anyway?

&

who are WE?

to begin with

GARDEN   (FOR ISAMU NOGUCHI)

a boy is born
of a swimmer & a poet

he hears nature's voice
in a perfectly split peach
& he dictates sounds of a brook

a dead bird can not
scare him

for he sees all

AND. TODAY. TOO.   (THE PRINZHORN COLLECTION: TRACES UPON THE WUNDERBLOCK)

I feel a tremendous pity for myself being part of this tinted cartoon strip that nobody reads. **And. Today. Too.** Just to welcome 8 variations of **HONOR**, I spread embroidered flowers all over the floor in my room. **Sole. Soul. Poodle. Bulldog.** I even paint a toad pond bathed in the imaginary light of full moon. *Come. Sweetheart, COME.* I love him and I hate him. I've written letter after a letter so he will not forget me and one day he might even answer my questions regarding the structures of those houses we built together. More than my desire to see him talk, I want him to feed my horse **TIME**. So, we, all, will be as free as torn clothes similar to plants from higher mountains I've heard of. **Dots. Cross. Gods.** How and when will they explain to me the map of the proof of **Divine Justice** against **Human Injustice**? I keep wondering. **Americolumbia. Africasia**, I am disembodied by **Cosmic Axis**, but I don't feel a thing. I just feel sweet. *Fairest one, meditate on bank notes.* Who is whispering? Who are you? Who is doing **Cain and Abel** on me? Insidious poisons allure me to believe that some mysterious murderous attacks are being prepared for me by the abandoned **Gods**. I know so well what's happening, but I enjoy pretending innocence. **Putt. Polka. Dots. Cross.** Follow me, just follow me sweetly through the color chart. Soon, before you know it, you'll be on my twentieth century calendar. Then, we'll all agree how **HONOR** helps. **And. Today. Too. Putt. Poodle.** *Come, Sweetheart, COME.*

MONDRIAN/FLOWERS   (AFTER STEVE)

a painter must have lent his ears to a breath of flowers

2 FOR ODILON REDON

I. THREE HEADS

one carried
one offered
one discarded

two with eyes shut
one with eyes open

one with words on its lips

night to night to night
day to day to day

a man listens for the fog to clear

all through history
the sea happens to end up being as it is
with the exception
of it returning to where
it comes from
to become air

II. THE WELL

to fall or rise

darkness & speed

wrap
around
your face

with a dreaming smile

3 FOR VERMEER

THE LOVE LETTER

a forest, framed.
an ocean, framed.

surprised by a love letter
handed to her unexpectedly,

a woman loosens
her five fingers on the neck of a lute.

the floor.
the wall.

being afraid that
everything in the interior of the room
might have seen
the violent waves
in her heart,

she murmurs,

"This must be a mistake!"

THE LACE MAKER

her hair touches her shoulders,
transparency makes patterns.

GEOGRAPHER

TIME pours itself down
through the glass window
into the eyes of a geographer
who loses himself totally

as he climbs the mountains,
crosses the ocean
& passes through the sky

it moves farther & farther forward,
going beyond its flatness,
surpassing its sharpness,
coming back to its flatness again

& muses on its own ETERNITY

POPPY FIELD   (MONET 1873)

"Mother!"

My voice has come up to here,
but I have held it back,
with respect,
listening to your silence.

I fully know
that I am still a young girl,
but I feel like I am as old as your mother,
following you
intensely staring at your back.

"Mother!"

How can I believe
that there is a happiness
in this world other than this one
of walking across the poppy field with you?

A fleeting remote blueness of the sky.
Painfully light clouds floating here and there.
A splendid density of small red flowers,
spreading all over, in front, back & sides of us.

What it means "to walk on water"
must be something similar
to this sensation,
wouldn't you agree?

A July afternoon always has the scent
of some tender hearted lonely person
burning a dry melancholy.

"Mother!"

Are you enjoying the vastness of summer
as much as I am,
being carried away
by a delirium?

For all that,
my heart aches.
An overtly remote past.
An overtly remote future.
I pray to my tiny heart
so that this joy of walking
together with you in the poppy field
will never end.

"Mother!"

Shall we make a garland?
Or shall we make a bouquet
big enough to fill our arms
to arrange them later
in a white vase?

A faintly winding country path
carries us who hide beneath
a parasol & a summer hat

quietly

&

composedly.

MUSÉE RODIN

*Pur(e). Impure. P(o)ur. Moi. Purring. Pur-*ring. Shapes of pleasure. Human faces/figures/bodies. A center called a torso which manifests the metaphysical reality of *Human Existence.* The right of speech, of bone structures, muscles & skin. Cosmos inside the skin. A non-lingual territory which connects an individual to the cosmos. *Eternity* floats up to the surface of matter. A fleeting fragility of shining dews.

Instead of paying attention to the art he created, I pay more detailed attention to the house where the artist & the poet lived; the place supported their daily routines. They must have stared at these walls & their floral patterns absent-mindedly on & off. I look at the wood grain patterns of the floors they walked on. I stand by the window where the world outside opens brightly. Doors, a simple wooden matter, separating one room from another, give a special right to solitude. Opening(s) & closing(s) of the door. Its repetitious gestures & sounds. I rest my eyes on the chairs whereupon they rested the foundations of their thoughts. Finally & slowly, I merge myself into a gentle darkness floating all around the house. Drawers & chests where they kept clothes, & mirrors that endlessly reflected their whispers. *History, Words,* lamentations, *Silence* vanished in their muteness...

Passing through the house packed with people with their bodies wrapped in summer clothes, I walk out to the garden. Looking for words of a poet (of our time), I swallow my own breath in the midst of flatness of summer green... Note books (of m.l.b.)... Hanako...

"The Gates of Hell" is narrative & its extreme narrativity somehow negates poetic emotions of the summer day we are breathing. A sudden gust & again a return to the ordinary.

UNTITLED   (FOR PHILIP GUSTON)

how long has it been
since this wall was
repainted
the present color?

an ex*tension*/ex*tinction* of
various curved lines
concretizes itself flatly
into a caricatured human quality.

behind "thoughts,"
decorative words
dry up, totally & cruelly,
as if they were the reminder
of leftovers from an unfinished dinner.

in the distance,

history of woods breathes an untitled abstraction.

2 FOR JOSEPH BEUYS

7000 OAKS

I reflected my lips
on Beuys' corroded mirror.

.   .   .

Did it really take
one third of a second?

DIRECT DEMOCRACY

I.
I still can not decide
whether it is good or bad
that your bits & pieces
are framed in
fake-wooden squares.

II.
Nothing to decide.

Why can't we all just be
flora-loving fauna?

FOR MAGRITTE

A man with a hat wondered,

"It's very strange.

Why am I standing here,
especially with two hands
hard-fisted in my pockets?"

A man in a coat wondered,

"It's very mysterious.

Why am I staring at the world,
especially at the world
smoking in gray,
with my mouth
so tightly shut?"

A man standing straight up wondered,

"It's very serious.

Why am I standing
between a bird & a fish,
especially right in between
those two foreign matters,
bolt upright,
with my mouth so tightly shut?"

Time becomes a circulating wind,
leaving scars in the present.

Flattering smiles disappear into a man's hat.

A man with a hat eagerly wondered,

"Why am I wearing a hat anyway?"

A SACRED CUP   (FOR GRACIELA ITURBIDE)

an organ
with wings

a girl
with an old man's face

a man
with the mask of God

we all bite
into flesh & blood

as if they were made
of milk & sugar

with a view vanishing
into the horizon

we innocently raise
a sacred cup

to the sky

THE WORLD'S OLDEST SHIP   (FOR WILLIAM L. HAWKINS, WRITTEN IN THE MANNER OF A STORYTELLING)

When I was just born, they placed me in a cradle, deep inside the world's oldest ship & told me "Don't tell anyone about this ship; it's a secret!" I could not speak any words then, but I understood what they meant, so I kept a promise to bury the secret at the bottom of my soul, body & mind, tightly sealed all through my life.

Growing up in the world's oldest ship, soon I learned how to sing funny & brave sailors' songs & how to enjoy the uncertain sensations of floating on the waters. Moreover, I mastered the whole scale of human language without ever learning how to read & write. All I needed was my sweet twinkling star eyes, a nose, a tongue & my shining skin. A guiding spirit was kind to me; not knowing what direction to take has never been my problem.

I have been travelling all through my life all over the world in the world's oldest ship; being protected by the world's oldest wind; by the world's oldest sun, moon & stars; by the world's oldest mother & father; by the world's oldest destiny. Oh, I have seen so many things, heard so many songs sung, touched so many different soils, but I have never thought any of them were "strange" because everything I've seen & heard was filled with "wonder" in the most marvelous sense.

Once I saw a woman, almost naked, fly, merging herself into one with an untamed animal; she was gracefully decorated with wild flowers. Once I saw a man with a hat on walk into the past & the future at the same time. I remember it was a cold day.

Once I enjoyed watching the fierce deadly fight of "pride against pride" between a golden striped animal & a furry animal of darkness with wet burning eyes. Oh, what a fight it was!

Once I heard a lonely woman's voice overlapping the shadow of the bridge over a river in an old town. Once I was awakened before sunrise by the footsteps of a blue boar & a mountain animal with horns serenading the pre-dawn sky. Once I saw Mona Lisa's nose wrinkle a cranky wrinkle for some obscure religious reason. Once I saw a Ferris wheel cry out my name over & over again, so I wrote it as I heard it.

Once I was told that the moon was just a round ball of dust. Did we need to erect a flag there? Once in the midst of a deep forest, I almost fought with a giant lizard with a tongue of fire. More than once, I've seen the snowy sky turn gray, purple & red. I saw fear shade a child's greenest of green eyes. Oh, I'll never forget the zigzag rhythm of the stairway of some building going up to Heaven that I walked on one summer day.

Now I am old as old as the oldest ship in the world & they say that I am ready for a new journey. The world's oldest ship is thin & long, shaped like an eye brow of a woman who has swallowed too much of the bitter-sweetness of life. But it has an unusually strong mast made of joy & mystery intricately hand painted to sail along with.

I've been travelling all over the world in the world's oldest ship, being protected by the world's oldest waves; by the world's oldest songs; by the world's oldest wisdom, by the world's oldest story & the world's oldest echo.

I want to tell you to remember not to tell anyone about this ship because it is a secret between you & me. & let's not talk of happiness or unhappiness, good or evil because everything is meant to "be" & all we need is the pureness of our hearts. I'd better go, it's about time. I'm glad that we met & I enjoyed talking to you. Good bye, now. Good bye, my friend.

THE WORLD'S OLDEST SHIP II

Bear Tiger Alligator
Blue Boar Reindeer Clouds & More
We Are All Privately Framed & Decorated
With Snow Flakes & Fruits
Scattered Around

Our Century Is Ferris Wheeling Away
As I Carve The World's Oldest Ship

INTRA-VENUS   (FOR HANNAH WILKE & LONA FOOTE)

hair forms clouds
weaving sighs
dancing a deforested seduction
to show us
the biological evidence
of your physical segments

.

see-sawing
in a sense of metaphysics

.

wearing a new hat on,
you brush your hair
in order to denote
the inner voice
hidden in your hand

&

your hand becomes
a lucid icon

you almost want
to kiss it
with respect
for the grand loyalty
you have toward

your own physical
existence

"my hand—
my rainbow hand
my fingers
my nails—
all joined
so perfectly—"

.

just for the fun of it
you stand naked
with a vase full of
pretty flowers
on your head, then,
you become a goddess, Venus
you smile, you laugh

& that's plenty

.

hair falls like
a water fall
& you glance
at the world
through the curtain of
an illuminated euphemism

& think

"I am not thinking
I am just looking,
don't you see?"

.

push down & turn
open & close
finish all
no refills—

if you swallow your chronicle
with food & milk
twice daily
you will one day
be labeled as
"caged-sugar-cubes"
& history
will applaud you
as loud as
it can afford to
so "why not sneeze?"

.

day to day
minute to minute
second to second
time to timelessness
you witness

your physicality
assaulted & forced
to segregate you
from you
& you realize
that you have been
such a good mannered observer
of your own detailed map
all these years

is it your eyes that we are facing?
is it your navel that we are looking at?
is it your thighs that we are marveling at?

.

see-sawing
in a sense of metaphysics

.

an ocean
an honor
a mother to all
a muse
a cook—

with a skinned tongue
sticking out
you make a face
at the world
just to show everyone

how a raw road leads
to the bottom of the well
where all those inspirations
for life pour out

as if they were refracted rays
through the mist
your cotton-filled nostrils

breathe the abstraction
of red, yellow & blue
when you try to say

something

.

from time to time
a bath tub cradles
your faint breaths
& your clear heart beat

you feel sleepy
for an instant
when you become

one

with

you, again

.

a dark victory
a camouflaged victory
massive dark soil
deep water—

musing with yourself
you pose as if
you were an object
for an aesthetic standard
of humanity

but even at this moment
you are constantly aware
of the blood & guts world
underneath your smooth skin

"let's have a ball
on my bone-marrow-harvest day!"

you even joke

.

see-sawing
in a sense of metaphysics

.

a river
a morning

an ecstasy—
laced underwear
half-covered &
half-uncovered
your nipples & areolas
& the image you create
are never just a metaphor
for an obscure desire
to be conquered

a luster
a monument
a flower petal—

remember that

to be or not to be

in the Origin

the sun was a woman

STAIRWAYS   (FOR EDWARD HOPPER)

Staring intently

at the way
the darkness of the forest
becomes one

with the space around it,

I quietly
climb down the stairs

to go outside.

Ah.

"Nothingness,"
residing beyond the rooftops,
sways trees
& we humans call those masses "a forest."

A woman,
a man,
a dog.

& a house.

The fact that there is no other way
but to "assume" "it" in order to know
the origin of every other voice besides mine
brings you & me

farther closer.

Walking down stairs,

verifying each step
I go outside

to become one with
a forest

myself.

FOR A GIRL WHO CRIES   ("TEARS" BY MAN RAY)

Teardrops; eye balls; tips of your eye lashes

are equally spherical

Your eye brows; eye bolt, eye beam; eye dialect

are definitely eye-catching

AN ARTIST WHO HAD A LONG NAME: A FOUND POEM FOR PICASSO

Pablo Diego José Francisco de Paula Juan Nepomuceno María de los Remedios Cipriano de la Santisima Trinidad Ruiz y Picasso

I LOST MY SHADOW (FOR AN INSTANT)

for date-unknown drawings by J. M. W. Turner, water-damaged but recovered from the Thames flood at the Tate Gallery in 1928

a face deformed,   with
        hands becoming air,
            a belly shipwrecked,

      but still   standing,

      I am an arched torso:
           a twisted glance.

      In brush strokes of void,
           sleep is levelled by
                the blank liquidity of wavelets.

      particles of river join
           the fate of
                a powdered storm
on covered, discovered, recovered   horizon.

         what is *"time"* in the midst of an ephemeral skin
                          such as this?

an artist, his models, all gone—

      finally history becomes
           a leaf of dark matter.

CODA

CLOUD STUDY: A FABLE   (CONSTABLE 1822)

BE be.

with each other's help,
it's all falling into place.

clouds
form
in nothingness
where no one feels awkward
following the footsteps
of a man who ate nothing but air
while he prayed for
PEACE & independence.

(a) Monk, (a) Bird, (a) Bud, (a) Doctor, (a) Prez, (a) Lady (Day),
(a) Colt(rane), Butterflies, Miles
& more.

muse–alchemists of sound/color/letters
from east, west, north & south
coexist harmoniously
holding a small remnant of a Navajo sand painting
as keepsake.

there, through all seasons,
Emily's voice humbly trembling,
like a clear faint bell,
announcing the dawn,
declares:

"I dwell in Possibility—"

in such GRANDNESS of nothing,

you & I kiss each other
in front of an arena
of the ruined architecture
of power & blood,

trying to erase
our memories
of the past.

HAIKU

spring rain—
did it fall
on Cezanne's pines too?

NOTES

p. 39

"August" was written after *August Sander: People of the 20th Century, A Photographic Portrait of Germany.*

p. 45

"Painters of Reality" was written after *Painters of Reality: The Legacy of Leonardo and Caravaggio in Lombardy.*

p. 163

From the "Sunday Poems" series

p. 259

From PINK: "Paris Trilogy" Part II

ACKNOWLEDGMENTS

Some of the poems in this collection were previously published in the following publications:

Chapbooks: *A Sunday Afternoon on the Isle of Museum* (Sisyphus Press, Propaganda Press, second printing); *Arena; Cornell Box Poems; Fragile; Genesis; 6 for L.B.; 3 for Lucian Freud* (all from Sisyphus Press); *A Voice That Crawls In The Sky* (Creature Press); *Small Poems* (UDP)

Journals: *The Recluse; Book of Broken Pages; Maintenant; 6 x 6; The 22 Magazine; Zen Monster; Big Bridge; Upstairs at Duroc; LiveMag!*

Anthologies: *The OWS Poetry Anthology; The Brownstone Poets Anthology*

I'd like to express my heartfelt gratitude to the artists who inspired me to write these poems; for the loving support of friends at Ugly Duckling Presse, especially to Anna Moschovakis, my editor, who encouraged me to do this project and worked with me in perfect harmony all through the way; and to Ryan Haley, Emmalea Russo and Matvei Yankelevich for volunteering to do the proofreading; to my late parents who gave me the first creative spirit; to my family and friends; to steve dalachinsky, the love of my life, for sharing his life with me and to whom this book is dedicated.

Without all of you, this book would not have been born.

STUDY & Other Poems on Art
Copyright © Yuko Otomo 2013

ISBN 978-1-937027-18-6

Distributed to the trade by
SPD / Small Press Distribution
spdbooks.org

First Edition, First Printing

Designed and typeset by goodutopian
with the author

Cover design by the author

Printed and bound in the U.S.A.
by McNaughton & Gunn

Funded in part by a grant from
the National Endowment for the Arts

**NATIONAL
ENDOWMENT
FOR THE ARTS**

Ugly Duckling Presse
The Old American Can Factory
232 Third Street #E-303
Brooklyn, NY 11215

uglyducklingpresse.org